Disney
BIG-note
COLLECTION

ISBN 0-634-01761-6

Walt Disney Music Company
Wonderland Music Company, Inc.

DISTRIBUTED BY

HAL•LEONARD®
CORPORATION

7777 W. BLUEMOUND RD. P.O. BOX 13819 MILWAUKEE, WI 53213

Visit Hal Leonard Online at
www.halleonard.com

THE BARE NECESSITIES

from Walt Disney's THE JUNGLE BOOK

Words and Music by
TERRY GILKYSON

Look for the bare ne - ces - si - ties, the simple bare ne - ces - si - ties, for - get a - bout your wor - ries and your strife. I mean the

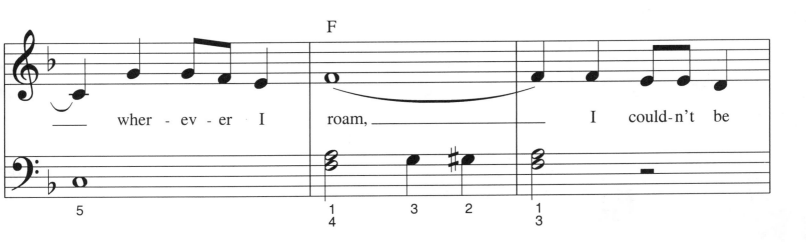

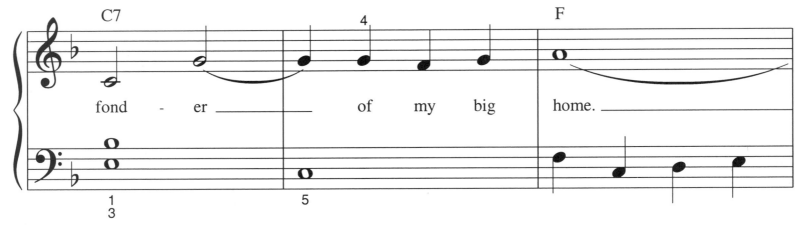

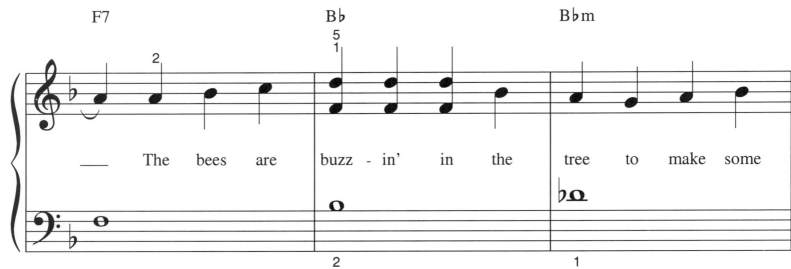

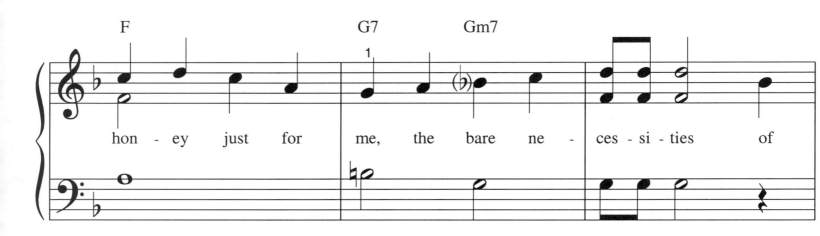

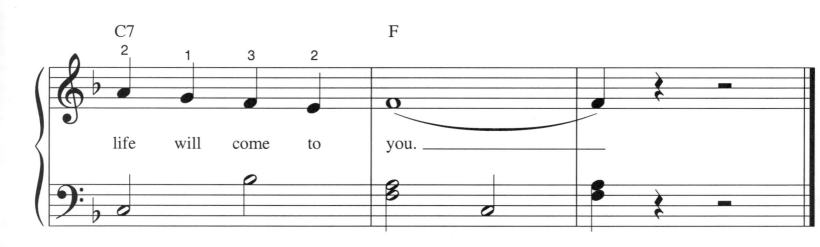

BIBBIDI-BOBBIDI-BOO
(The Magic Song)
from Walt Disney's CINDERELLA

Words by JERRY LIVINGSTON
Music by MACK DAVID and AL HOFFMAN

9

BEAUTY AND THE BEAST

from Walt Disney's BEAUTY AND THE BEAST

Lyrics by HOWARD ASHMAN
Music by ALAN MENKEN

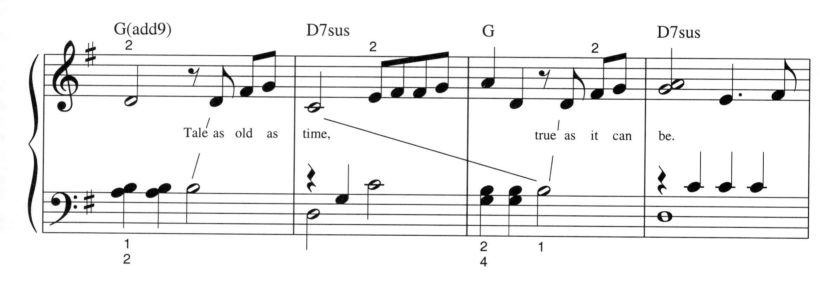

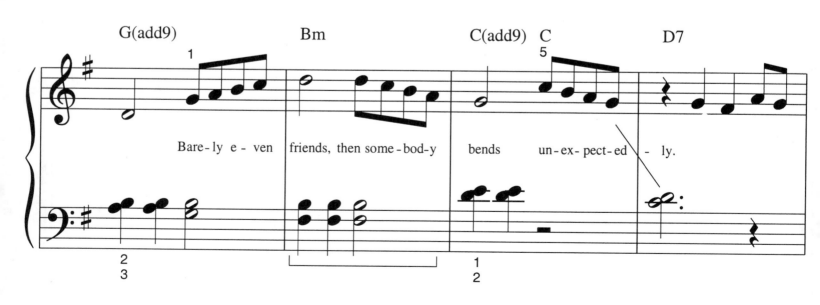

11

12

BELLA NOTTE
(This Is the Night)
from Walt Disney's LADY AND THE TRAMP

Words and Music by PEGGY LEE
and SONNY BURKE

CAN YOU FEEL THE LOVE TONIGHT

from Walt Disney Pictures' THE LION KING

Music by ELTON JOHN
Lyrics by TIM RICE

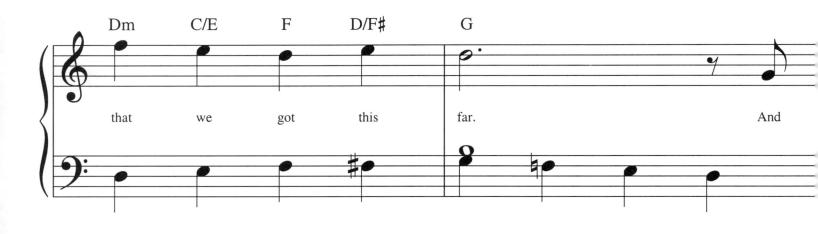

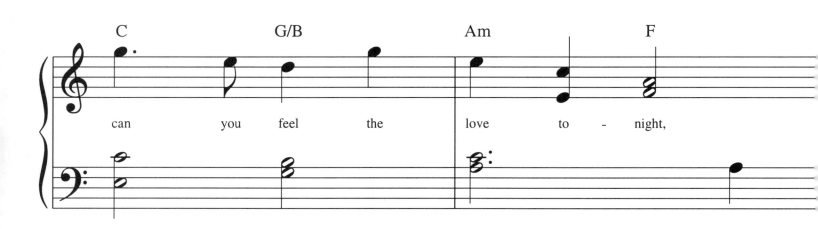

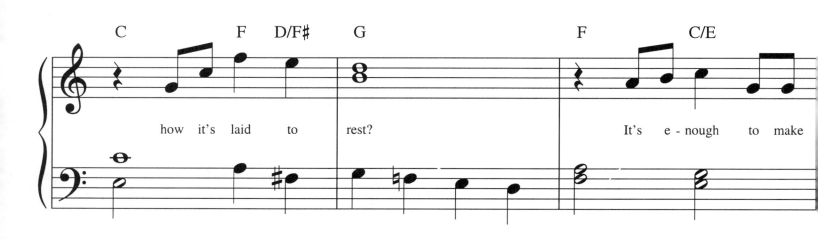

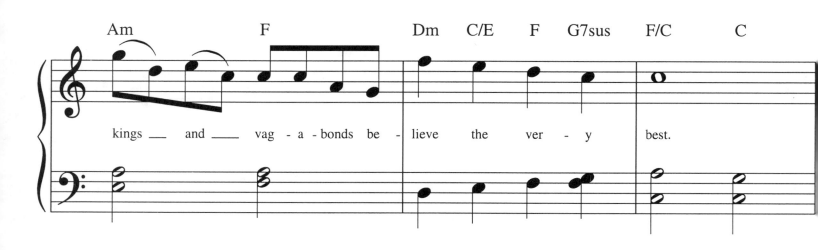

CANDLE ON THE WATER

from Walt Disney's PETE'S DRAGON

Words and Music by AL KASHA
and JOEL HIRSCHHORN

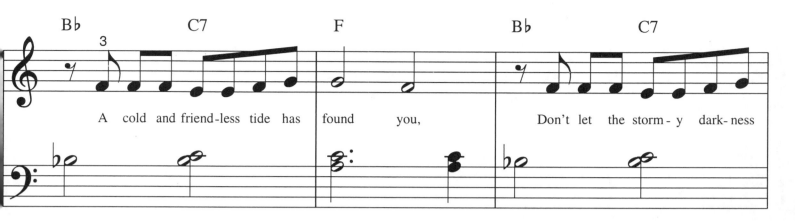

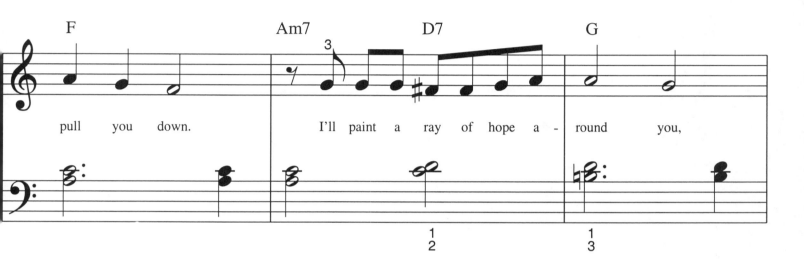

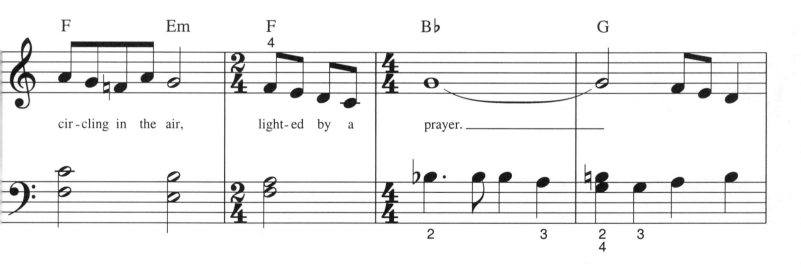

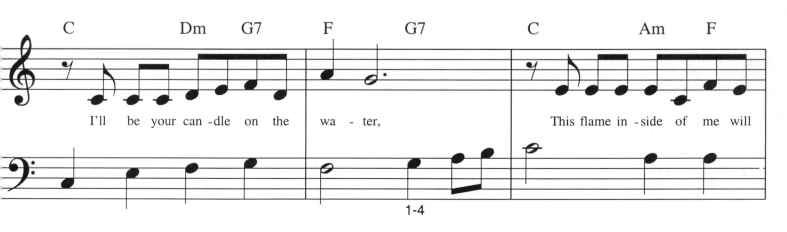

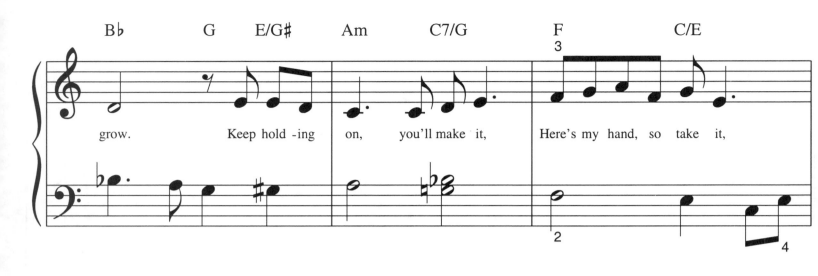

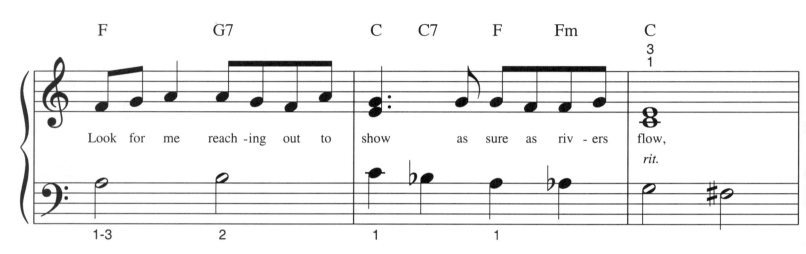

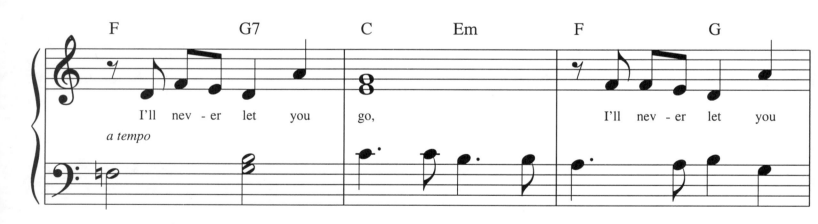

CHIM CHIM CHER-EE

from Walt Disney's MARY POPPINS

Words and Music by RICHARD M. SHERMAN
and ROBERT B. SHERMAN

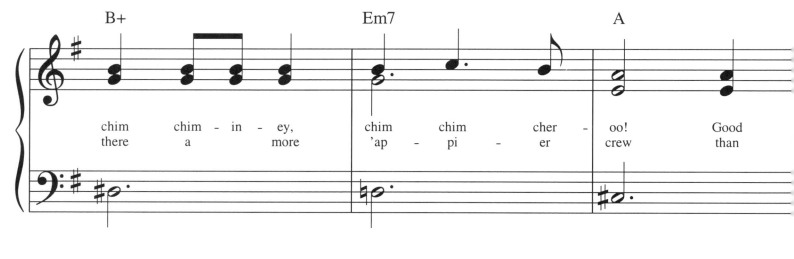

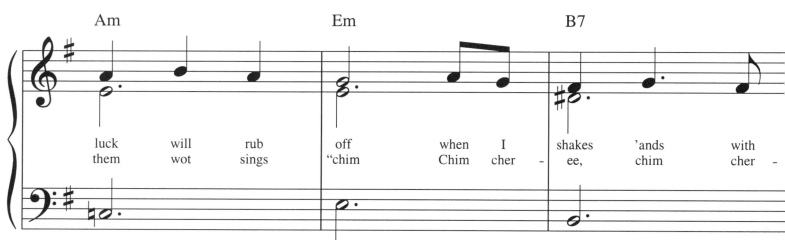

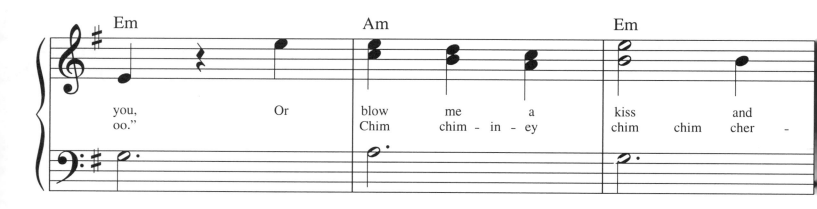

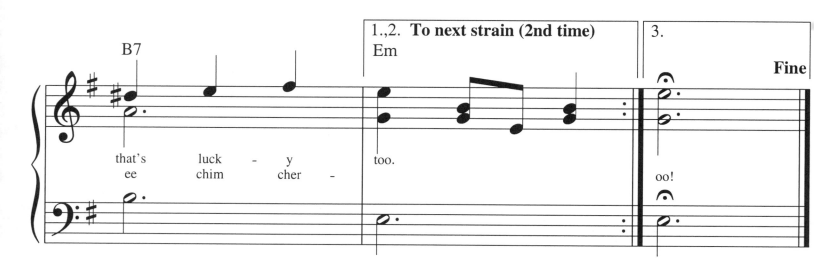

CIRCLE OF LIFE
from Walt Disney Pictures' THE LION KING

Music by ELTON JOHN
Lyrics by TIM RICE

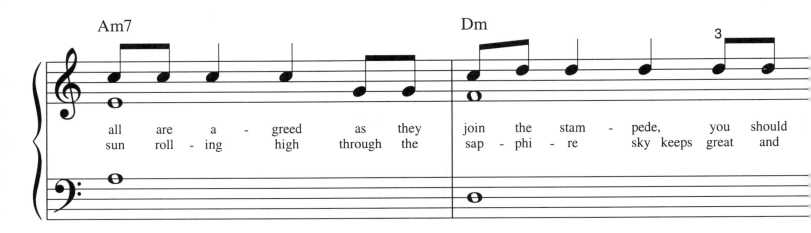

all   are   a - greed   as   they   join   the   stam - pede,   you   should
sun   roll - ing   high   through   the   sap - phi - re   sky   keeps   great   and

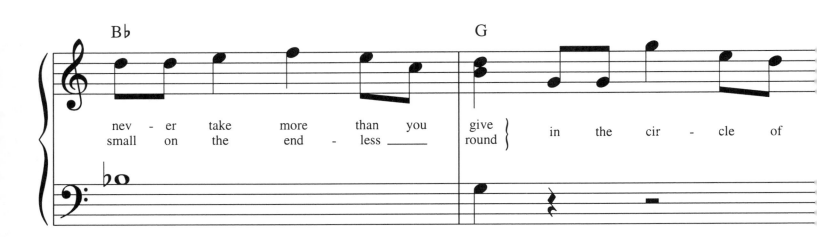

nev - er   take   more   than   you   give   in   the   cir - cle   of
small   on   the   end - less _____   round   }

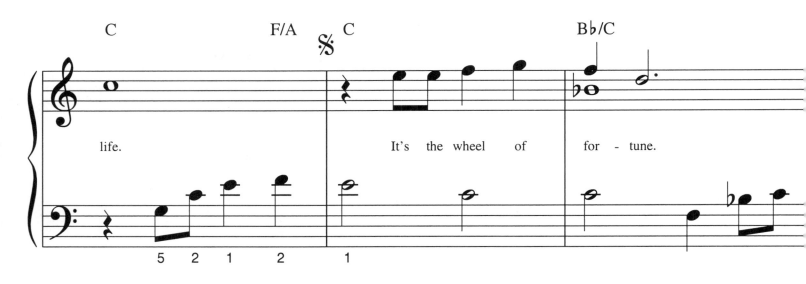

life.   It's   the   wheel   of   for - tune.

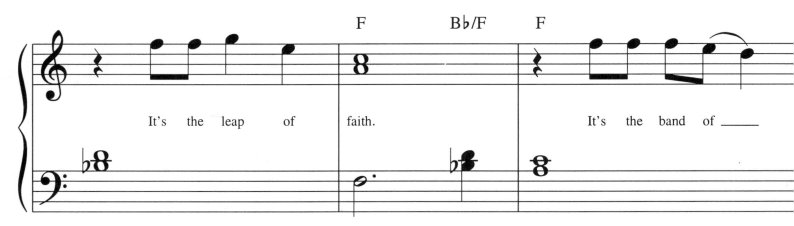

It's   the   leap   of   faith.   It's   the   band   of _____

COLORS OF THE WIND
from Walt Disney's POCAHONTAS

Music by ALAN MENKEN
Lyrics by STEPHEN SCHWARTZ

CRUELLA DE VIL

from Walt Disney's 101 DALMATIANS

Words and Music by
MEL LEVEN

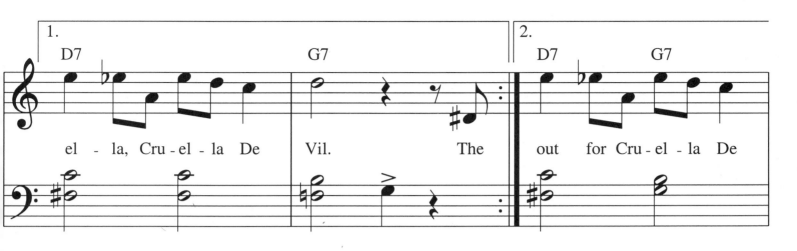

el - la, Cru - el - la De Vil. The out for Cru - el - la De

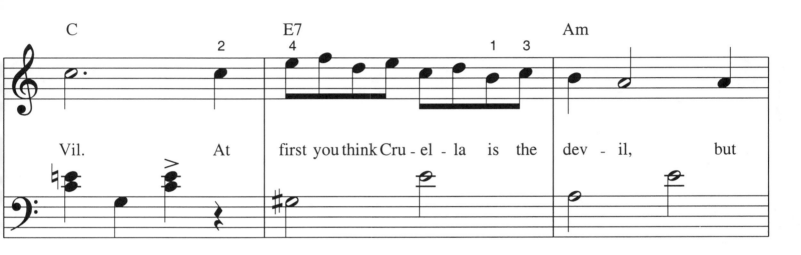

Vil. At first you think Cru - el - la is the dev - il, but

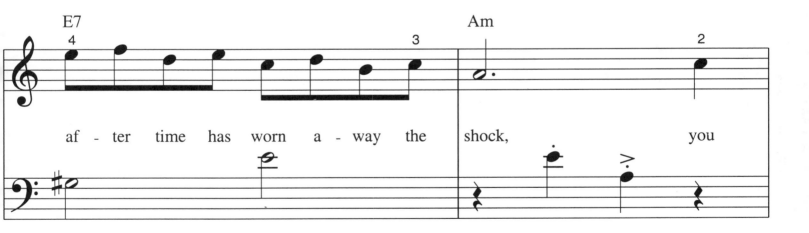

af - ter time has worn a - way the shock, you

come to re - al - ize you've seen her kind of eyes

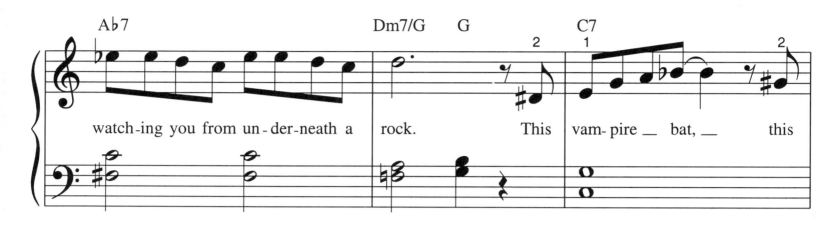

watch-ing you from un-der-neath a rock. This vam-pire __ bat, __ this

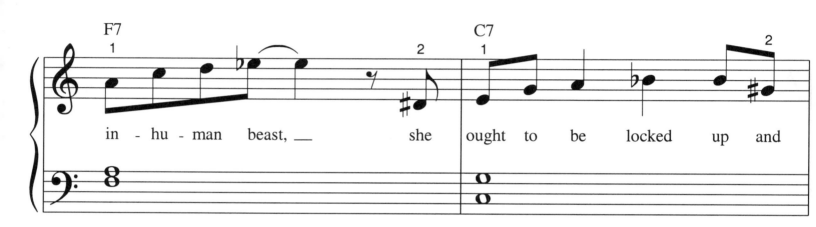

in - hu - man beast, __ she ought to be locked up and

nev - er re - leased. __ The world was such a whole-some place un -

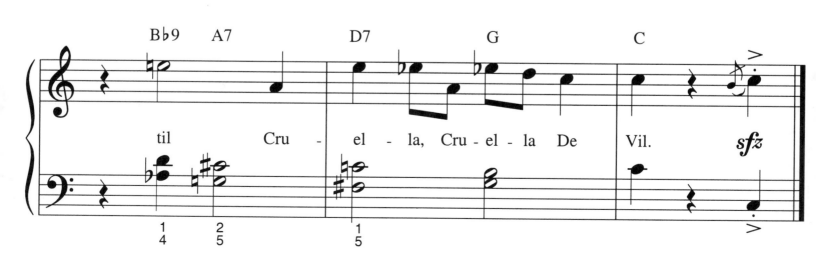

til Cru - el - la, Cru-el - la De Vil.

A DREAM IS A WISH YOUR HEART MAKES

from Walt Disney's CINDERELLA

Words and Music by MACK DAVID,
AL HOFFMAN and JERRY LIVINGSTON

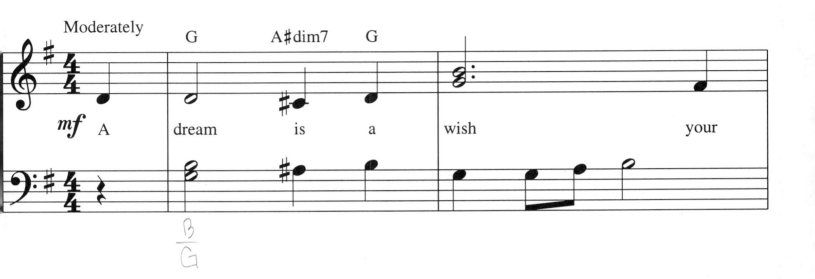

Am ... Am7

dreams you will lose your heart - aches; ___

D7

___ what - ev - er you wish for, you

G ... Am7 F+ D+ G A#dim7 G

keep. Have faith in your

dreams and some day ___ your

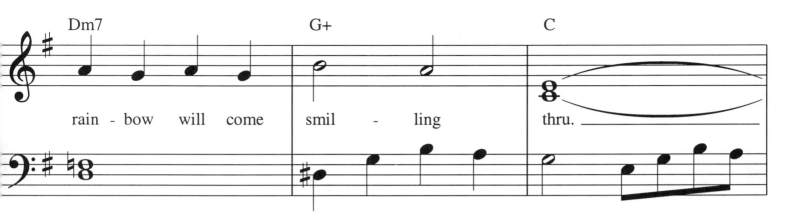

rain - bow will come   smil - ling   thru. _____

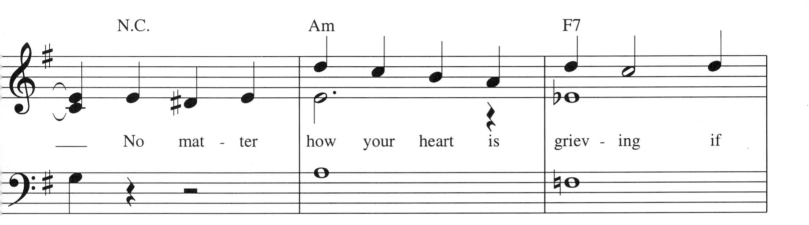

_____ No mat - ter   how your heart is   griev - ing   if

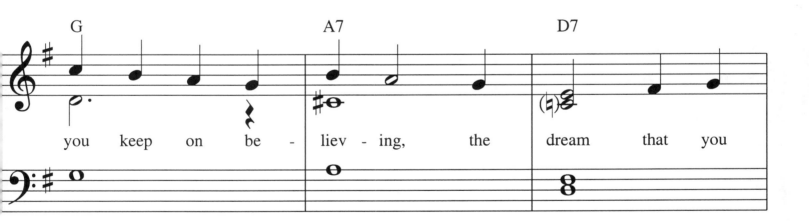

you keep on be - liev - ing,   the   dream that you

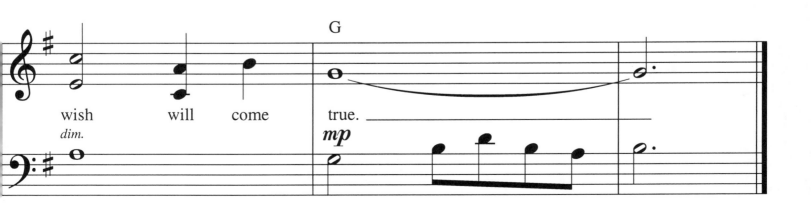

wish will come   true. _____

EV'RYBODY WANTS TO BE A CAT

from Walt Disney's THE ARISTOCATS

Words by FLOYD HUDDLESTON
Music by AL RINKER

47

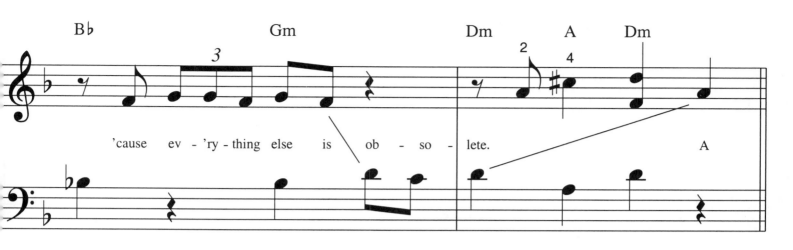

'cause ev – 'ry – thing else is ob – so – lete. A

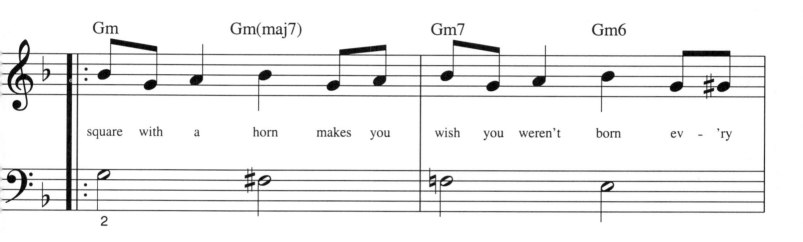

square with a horn makes you wish you weren't born ev – 'ry

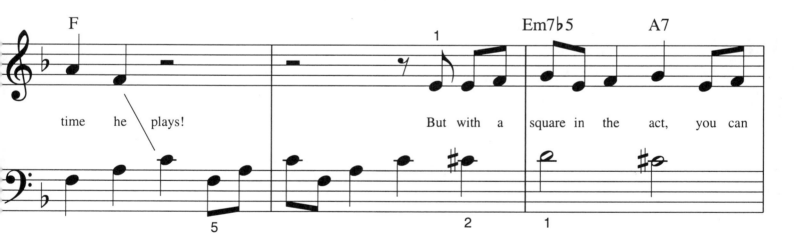

time he plays! But with a square in the act, you can

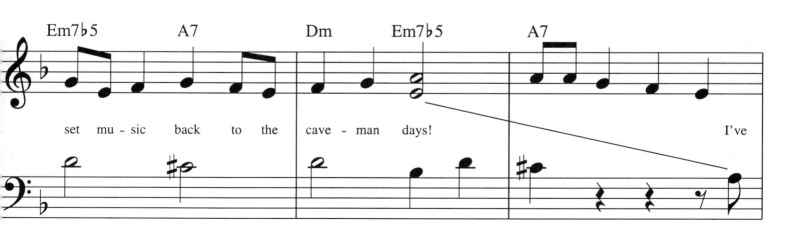

set mu – sic back to the cave – man days! I've

GO THE DISTANCE

from Walt Disney Pictures' HERCULES

Music by ALAN MENKEN
Lyrics by DAVID ZIPPEL

Young Hercules: I have

FRIEND LIKE ME
from Walt Disney's ALADDIN

Lyrics by HOWARD ASHMAN
Music by ALAN MENKEN

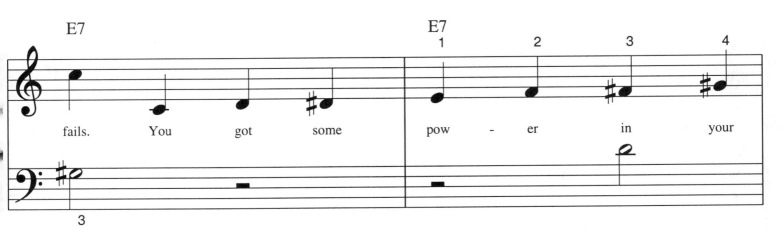

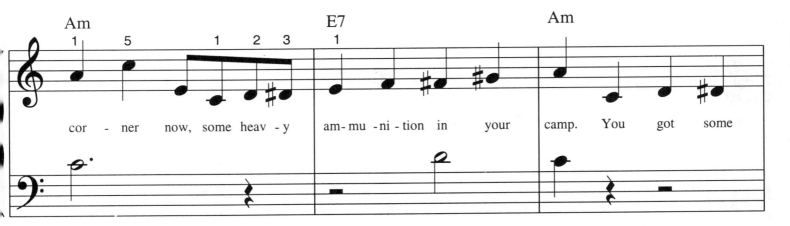

56

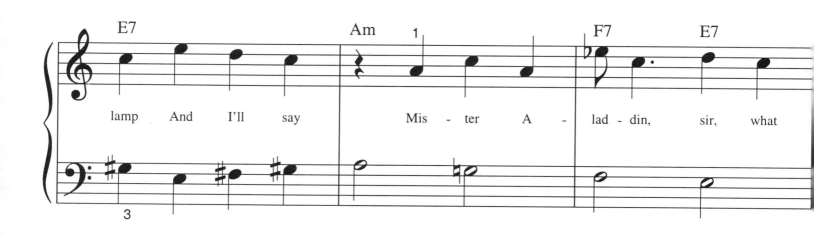

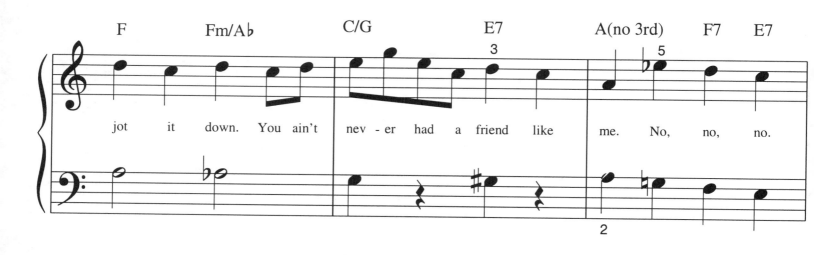

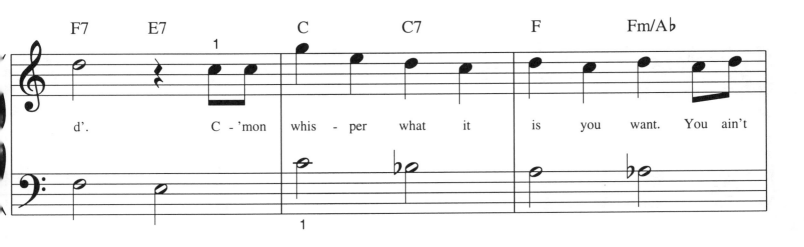

F7 E7 C C7 F Fm/A♭

d'. C -'mon whis - per what it is you want. You ain't

C/G E7 Am

nev - er had a friend like me. Yes, sir, we

F7   Am

pride our - selves on ser - vice. You're the boss, the king, the

  F7

shah. Say what you wish. It's yours! True dish how 'bout a

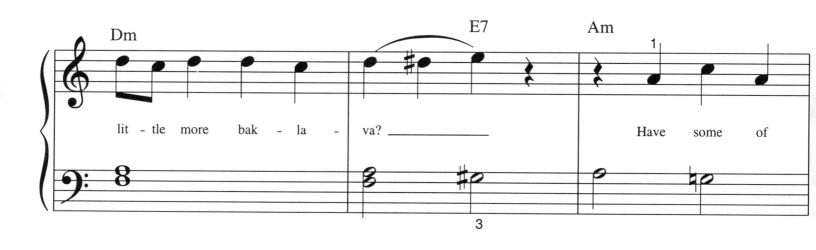

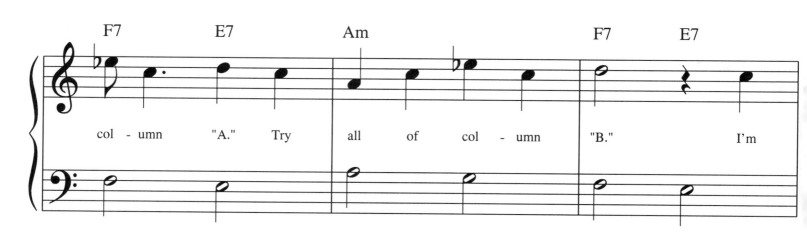

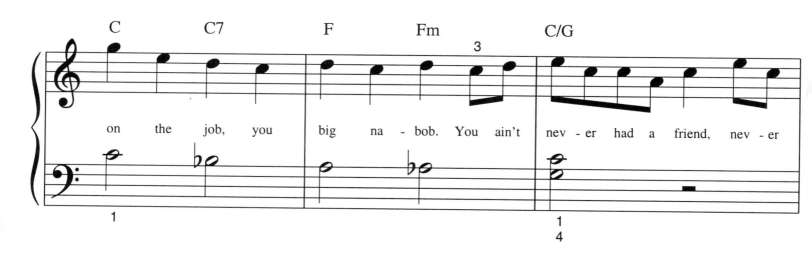

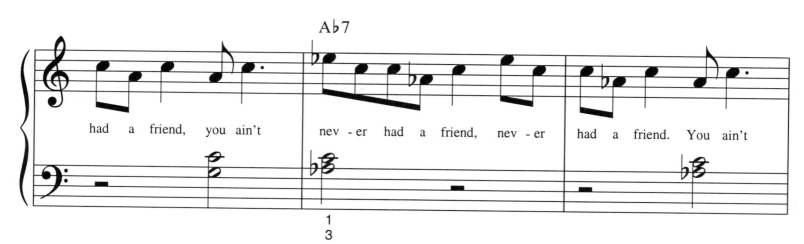

GOD HELP THE OUTCASTS
from Walt Disney's THE HUNCHBACK OF NOTRE DAME

Music by ALAN MENKEN
Lyrics by STEPHEN SCHWARTZ

62

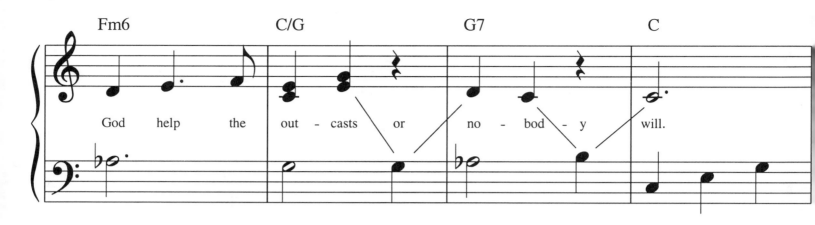

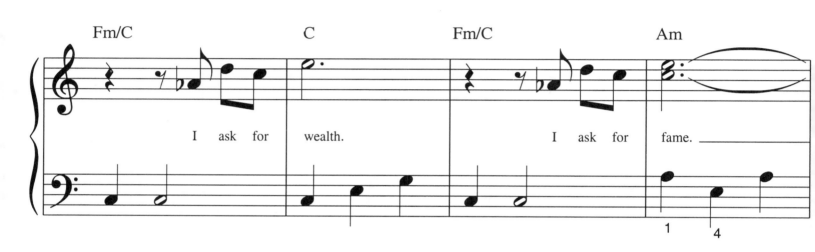

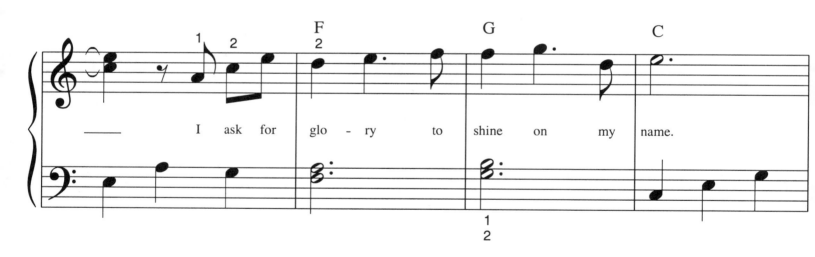

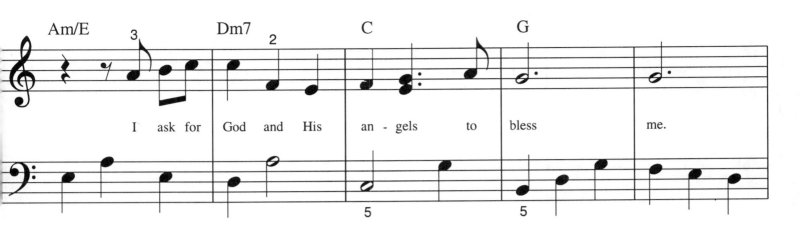

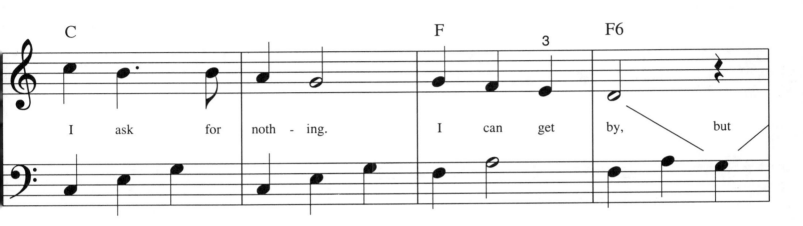

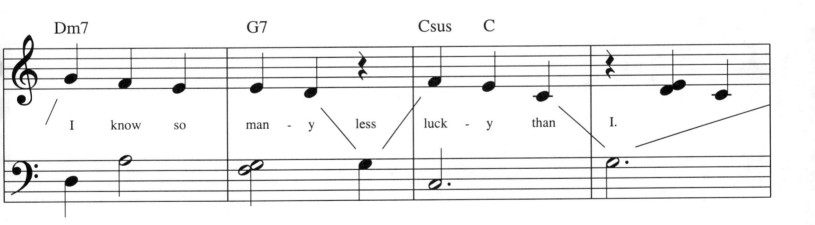

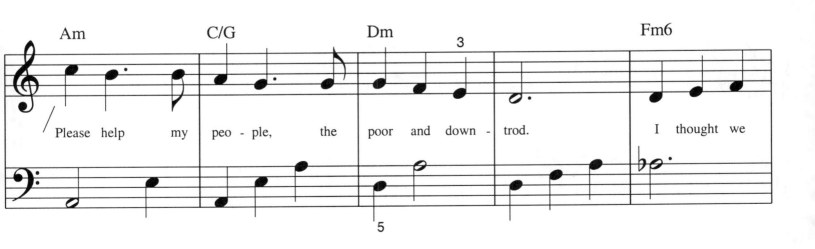

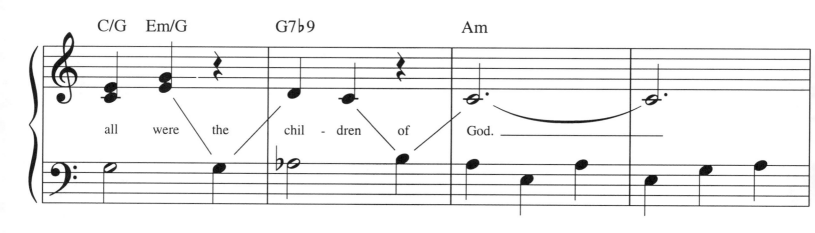

all were the chil - dren of God.

Slower

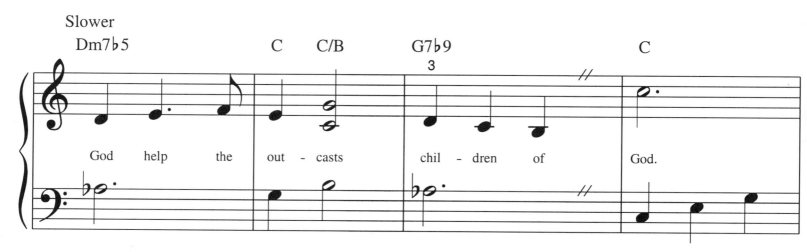

God help the out - casts chil - dren of God.

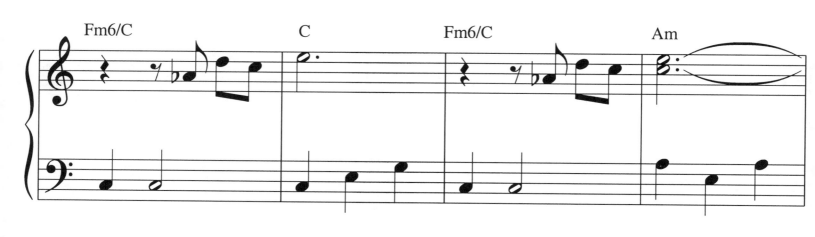

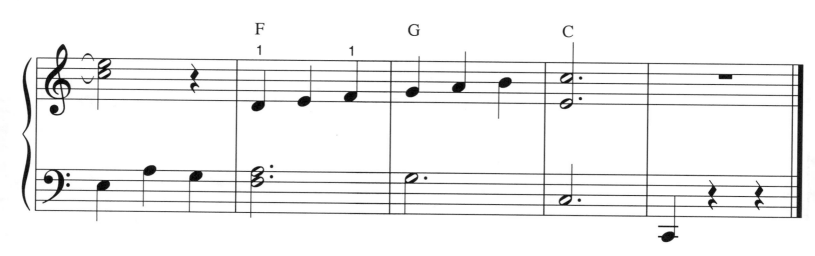

HAKUNA MATATA
from Walt Disney Pictures' THE LION KING

Music by ELTON JOHN
Lyrics by TIM RICE

70

I WAN'NA BE LIKE YOU

(The Monkey Song)
from Walt Disney's THE JUNGLE BOOK

Words and Music by RICHARD M. SHERMAN
and ROBERT B. SHERMAN

Brightly, with a jungle beat

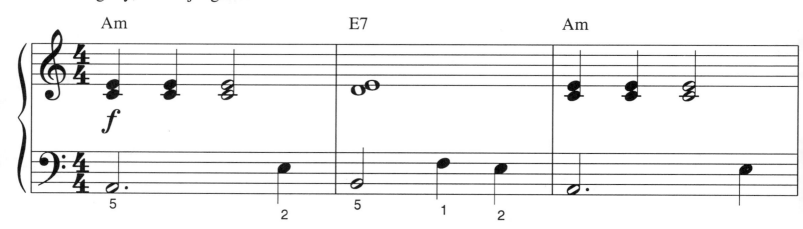

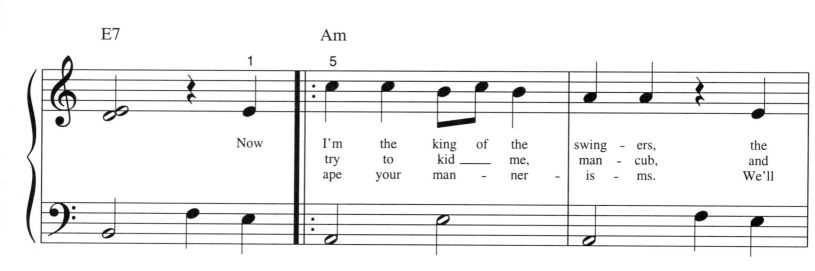

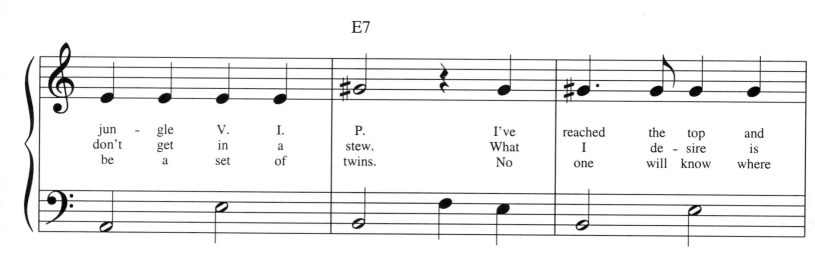

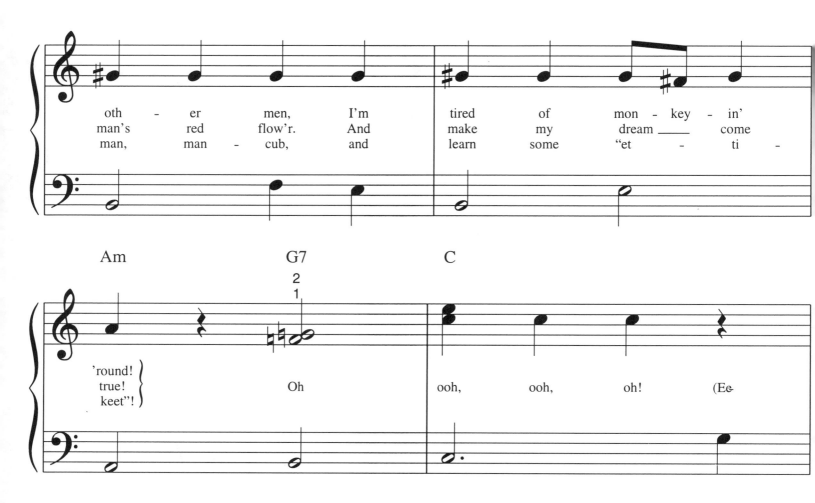

oth - er men, I'm
man's red flow'r. And
man, man - cub, and

tired of mon - key - in'
make my dream ____ come
learn some "et - ti -

Am   G7   C

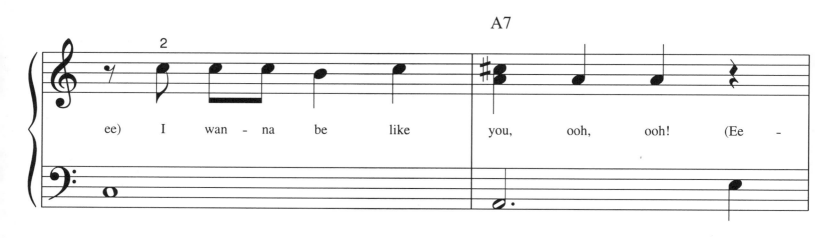

'round!
true!
keet"!

Oh   ooh,   ooh,   oh!   (Ee-

                               A7

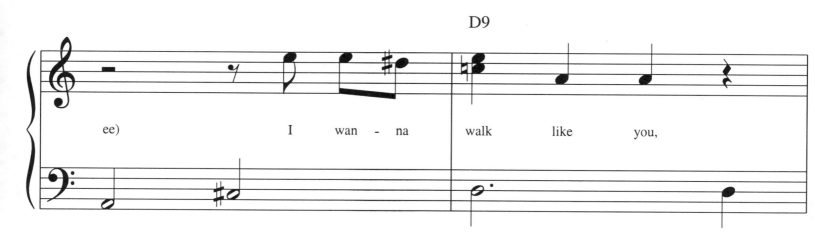

ee)   I   wan - na   be   like   you,   ooh,   ooh!   (Ee -

                               D9

ee)   I   wan - na   walk   like   you,

I'M LATE
from Walt Disney's ALICE IN WONDERLAND

Words by BOB HILLIARD
Music by SAMMY FAIN

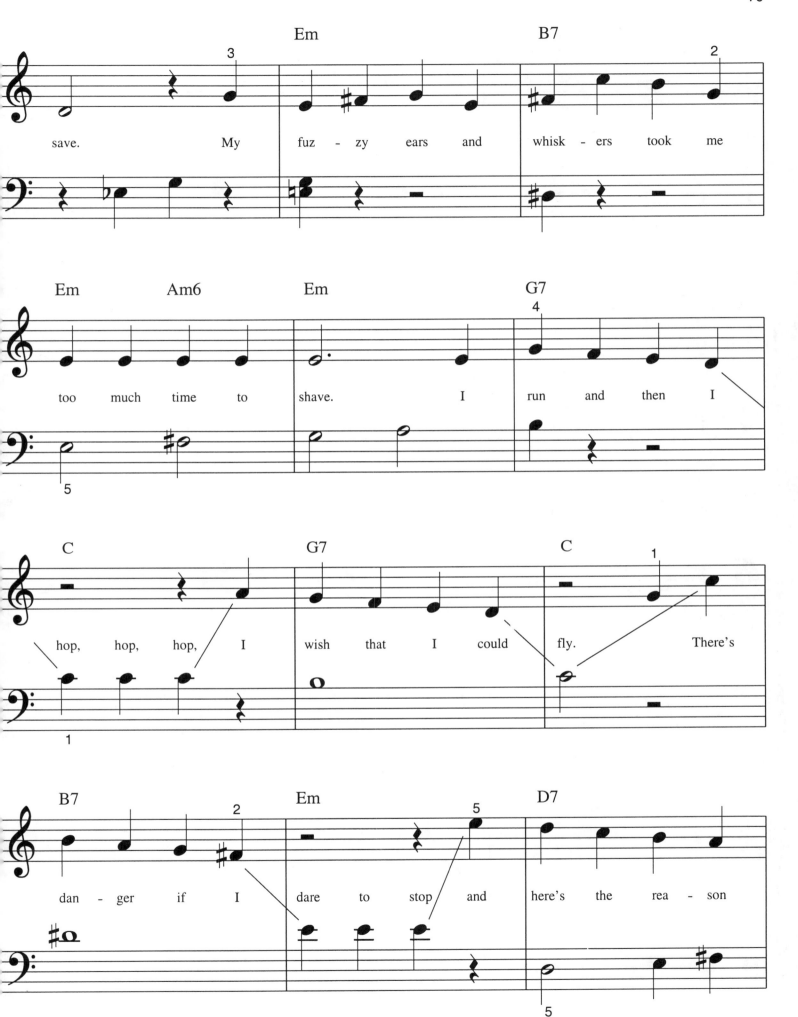

81

IF I NEVER KNEW YOU
(Love Theme from POCAHONTAS)
from Walt Disney's POCAHONTAS

Music by ALAN MENKEN
Lyrics by STEPHEN SCHWARTZ

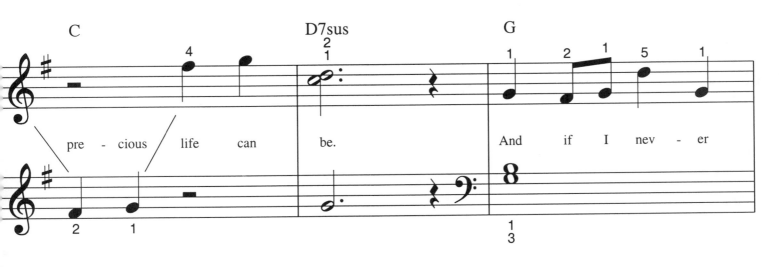

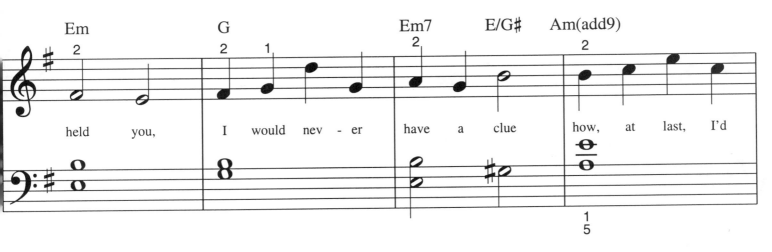

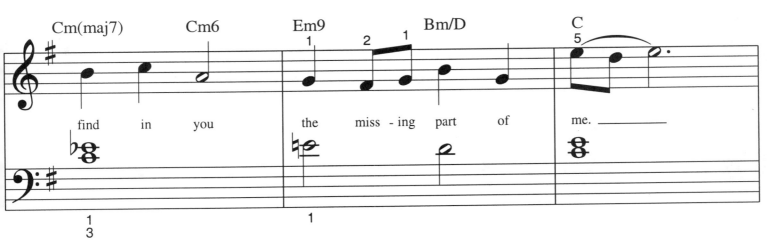

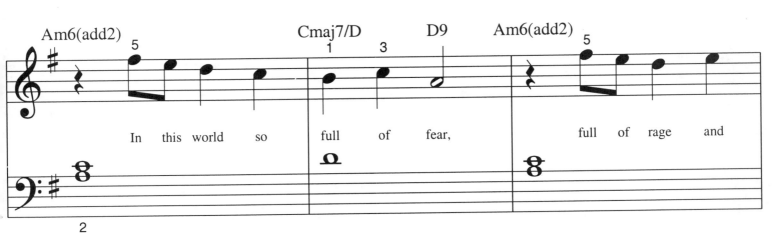

84

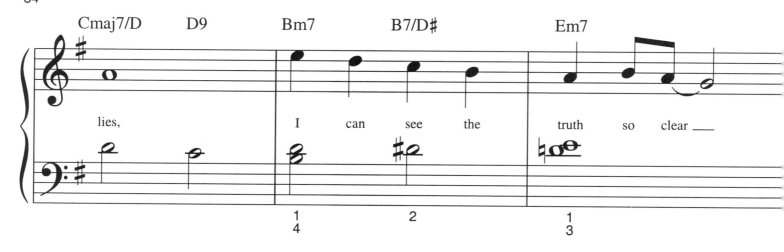

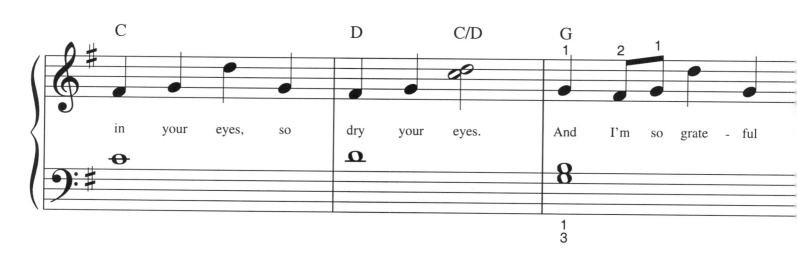

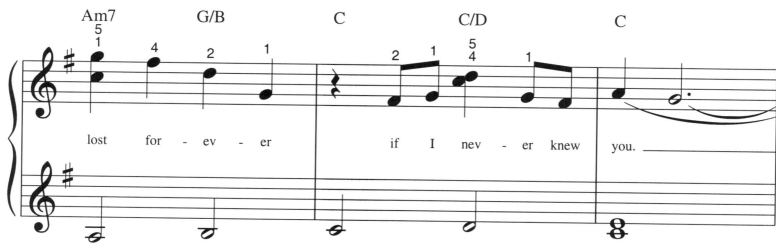

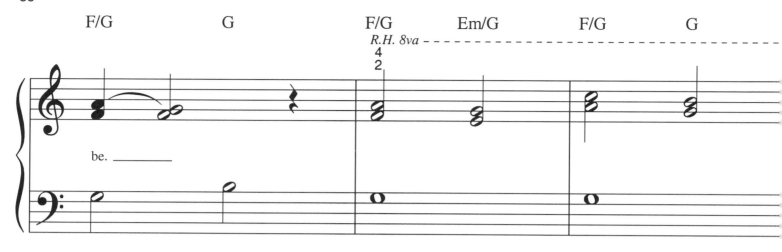

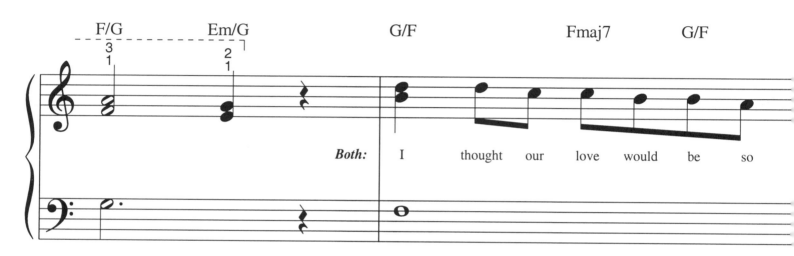

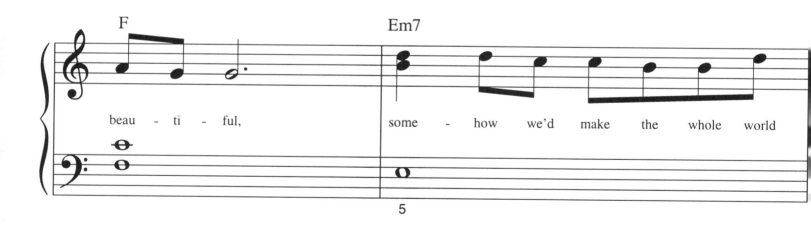

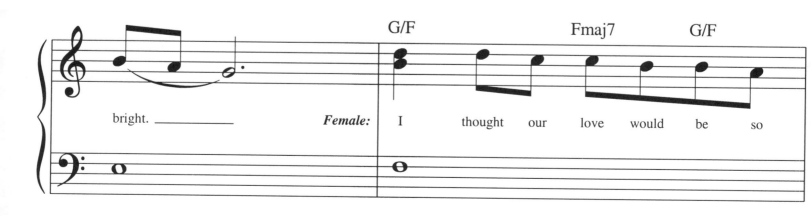

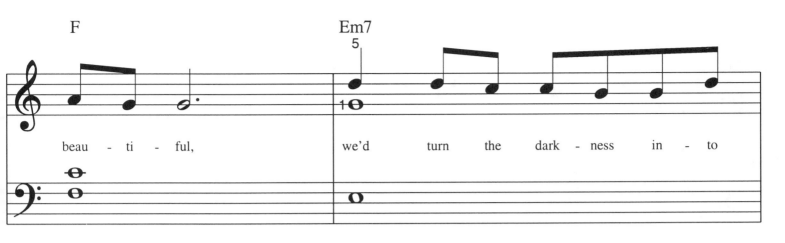

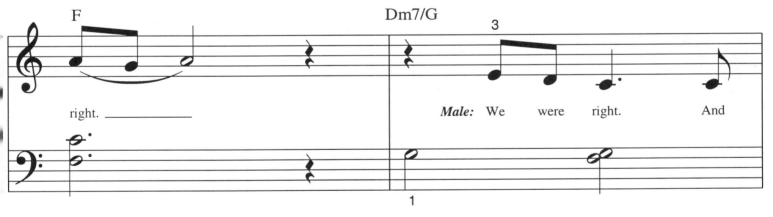

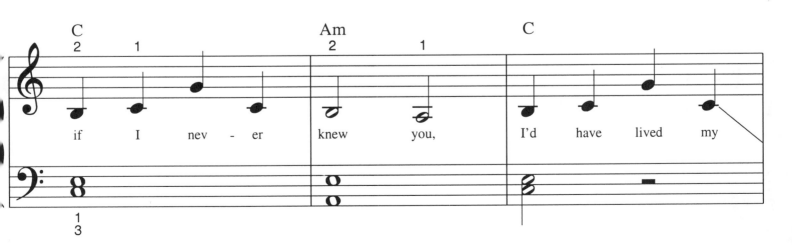

LITTLE APRIL SHOWER
from Walt Disney's BAMBI

Words by LARRY MOREY
Music by FRANK CHURCHILL

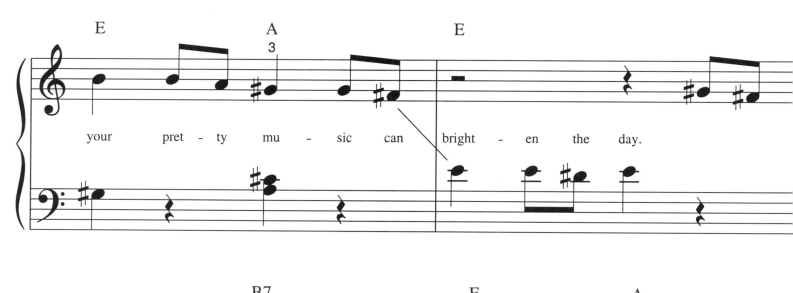

your pret – ty mu – sic can bright – en the day.

Drip, drip, drop, when the sun says, "How – dy"

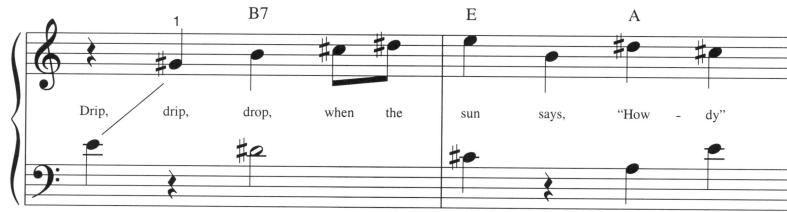

you say "Good – bye" right a – way. _____

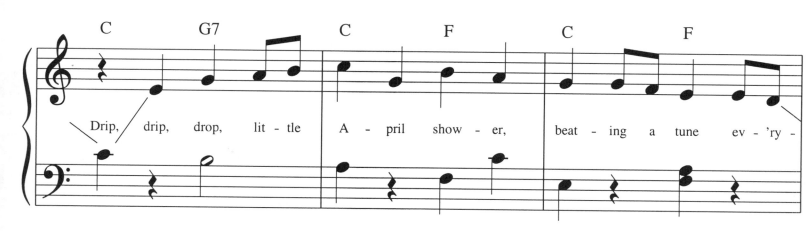

Drip, drip, drop, lit – tle A – pril show – er, beat – ing a tune ev – 'ry –

IT'S A SMALL WORLD
from Disneyland and Walt Disney World's IT'S A SMALL WORLD

Words and Music by RICHARD M. SHERMAN
and ROBERT B. SHERMAN

March Tempo

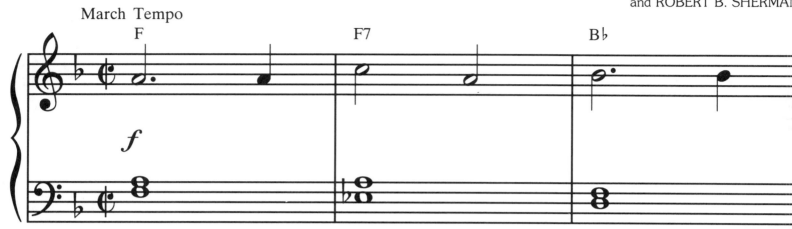

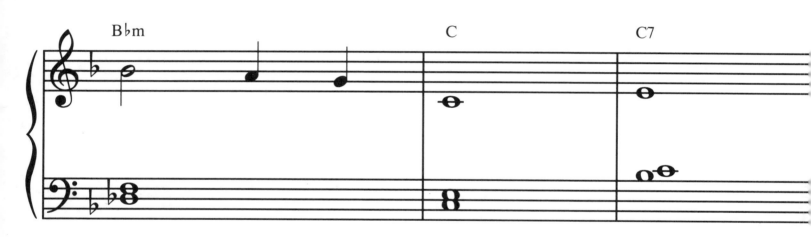

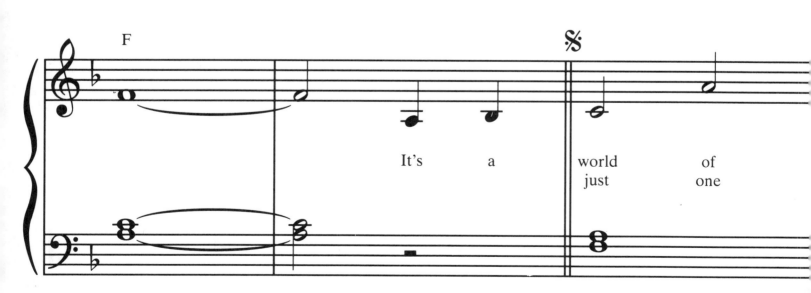

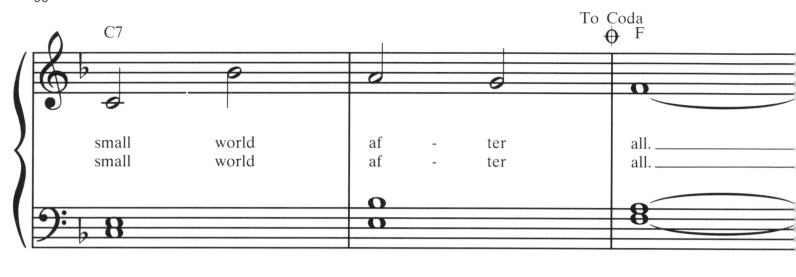

small world af - ter all.
small world af - ter all.

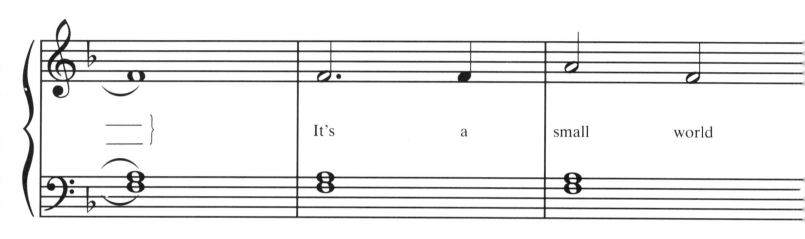

It's a small world

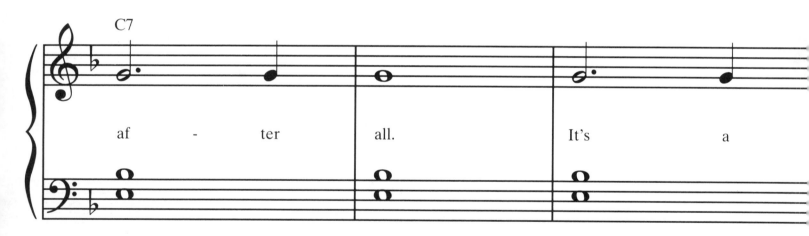

af - ter all. It's a

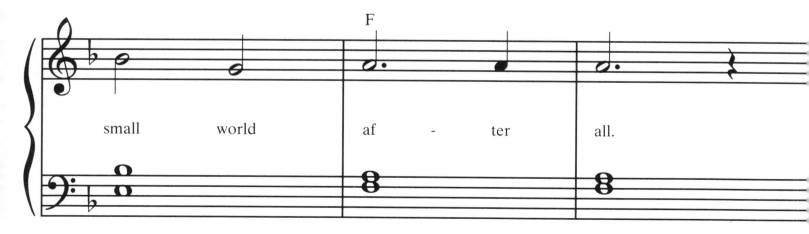

small world af - ter all.

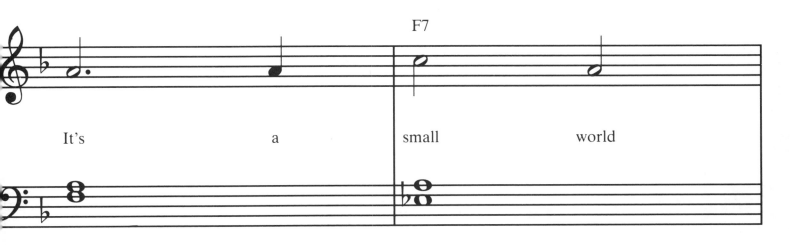

It's a small world

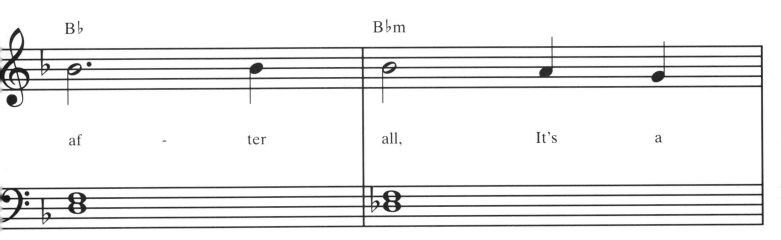

af - ter all, It's a

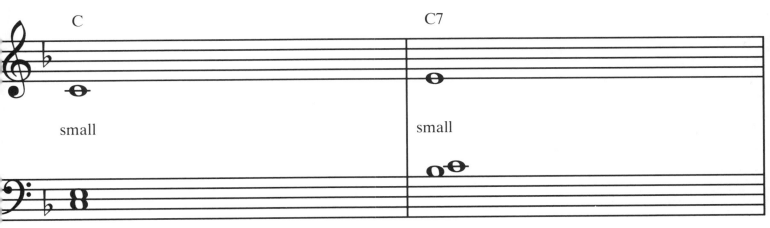

small small

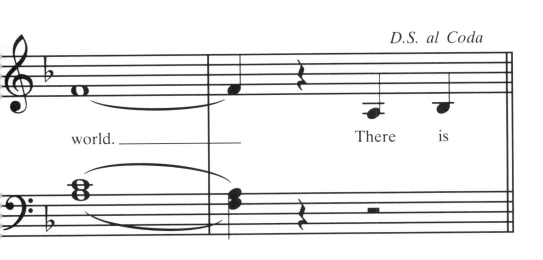

world. _____ There is

D.S. al Coda

CODA

all.

KISS THE GIRL
from Walt Disney's THE LITTLE MERMAID

Lyrics by HOWARD ASHMAN
Music by ALAN MENKEN

Moderately

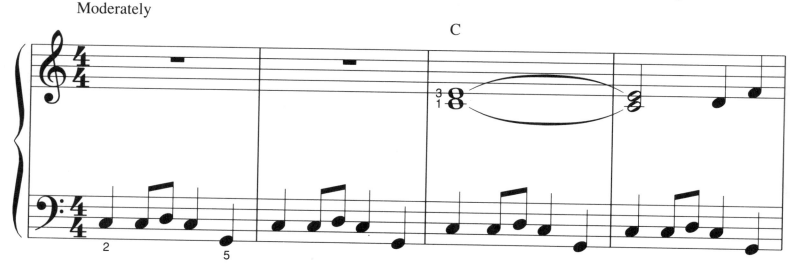

There you see her sit-ting there a-cross the way.

She don't got a lot to say, but there's some-thing a - bout her.

Now's your mo - ment, float-ing in a blue la -

LET'S GO FLY A KITE
from Walt Disney's MARY POPPINS

Words and Music by RICHARD M. SHERMAN
and ROBERT B. SHERMAN

Joyfully

THE LORD IS GOOD TO ME

from Walt Disney's MELODY TIME

Words and Music by KIM GANNON
and WALTER KENT

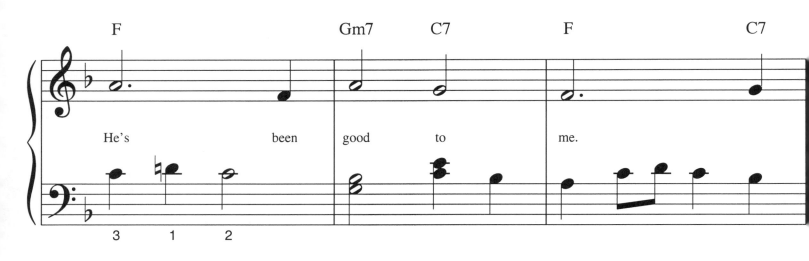

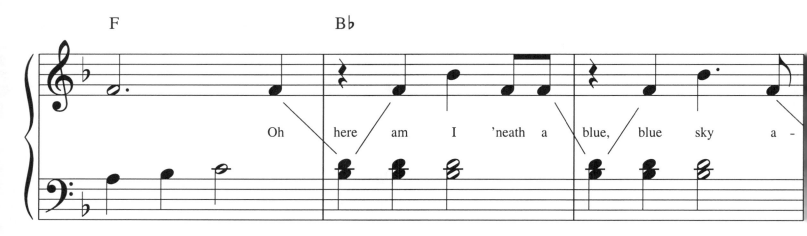

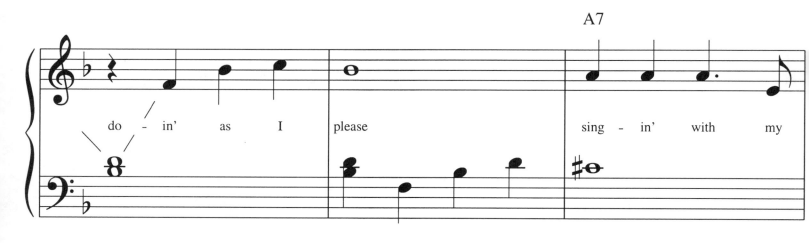

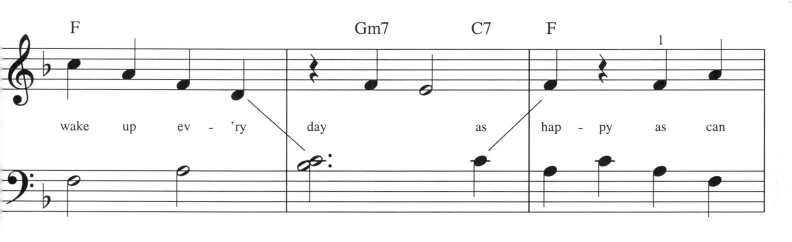

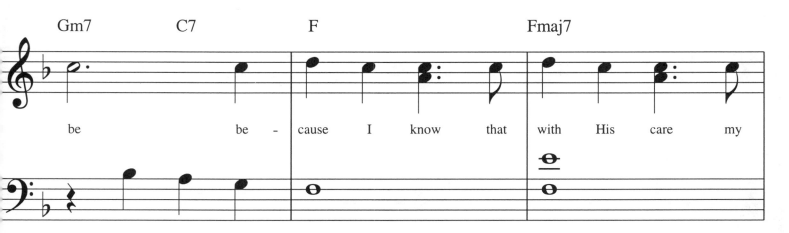

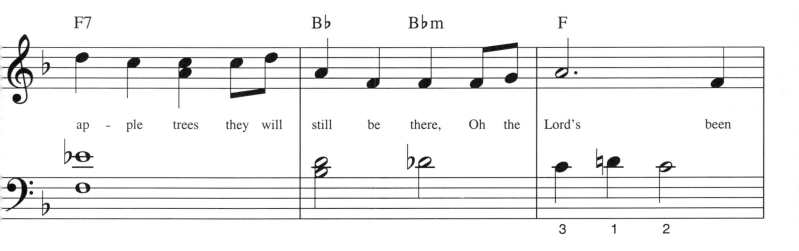

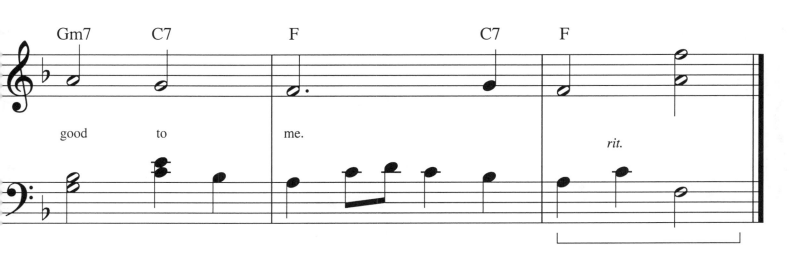

MICKEY MOUSE MARCH
from Walt Disney's THE MICKEY MOUSE CLUB

Words and Music by
JIMMIE DODD

Bright march tempo

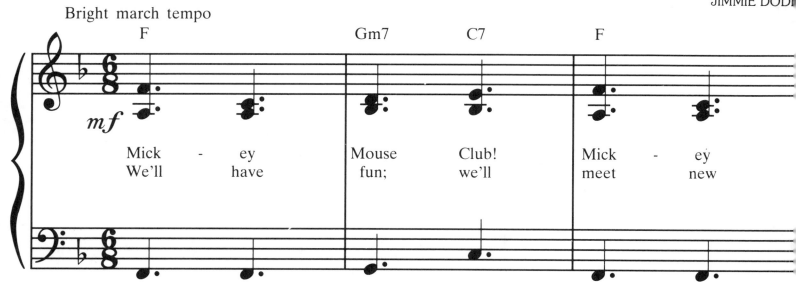

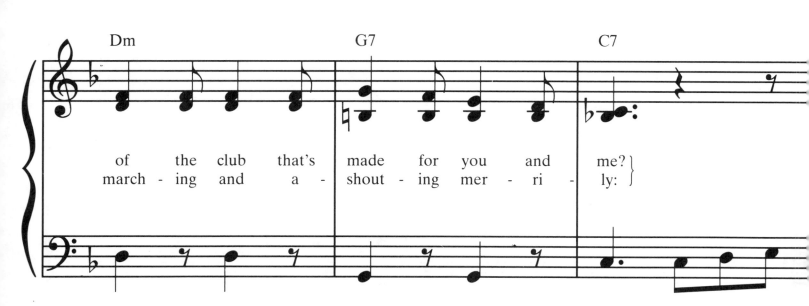

Additional Interludes

3. We'll do things and we'll go places!

4. All around the world we're marching!

5. We have fun and we play safely!

6. Look both ways when you cross crossings!

7. Don't take chances! Play with safety!

8. When you ride your bike be careful!

9. Play a little, work a little.

10. Sing a song while you are working!

11. It will make your burden lighter.

12. Do a good turn for your neighbor.

13. You can learn things while you're playing.

14. It's a lot of fun to learn things.

NEVER SMILE AT A CROCODILE

from Walt Disney's PETER PAN

Words by JACK LAWRENCE
Music by FRANK CHURCHILL

G7

mag - in - ing how well you'd fit with - in his skin.

C7

1
2

F

3

Nev - er smile at a croc - o - dile, Nev - er

B♭

tip your hat and stop to

F

talk a while { Nev - er
Don't be

B♭　　　　**F**　　　　**B♭**　　　　**F**

run, Walk a - way, say "Good - night" not "Good day!" } Clear the

rude, Nev - er mock, Throw a kiss, Not a rock. }

116

REFLECTION
from Walt Disney Pictures' MULAN

Music by MATTHEW WILDER
Lyrics by DAVID ZIPPEL

PART OF YOUR WORLD
from Walt Disney's THE LITTLE MERMAID

Lyrics by HOWARD ASHMAN
Music by ALAN MENKEN

Moderately bright

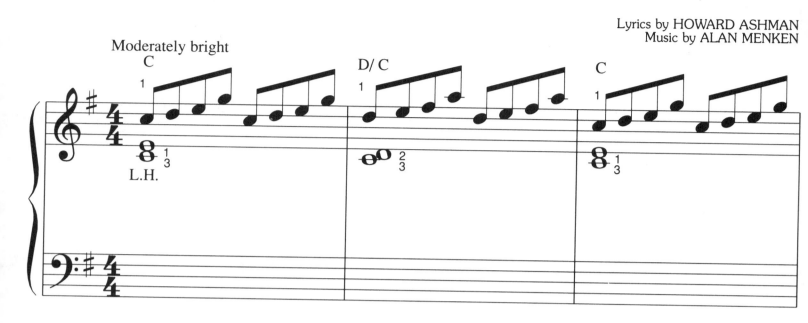

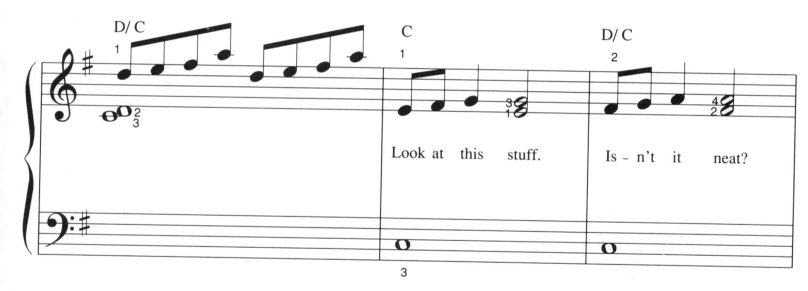

Look at this stuff. Is - n't it neat?

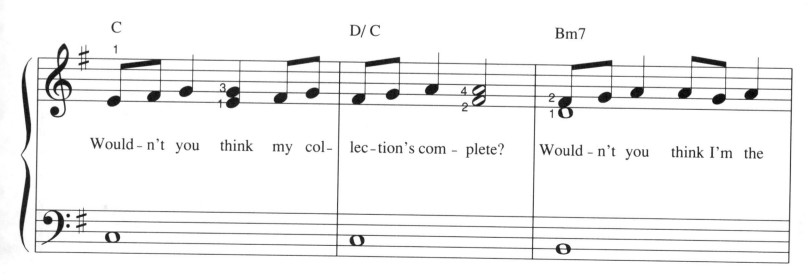

Would – n't you think my col- lec -tion's com – plete? Would – n't you think I'm the

121

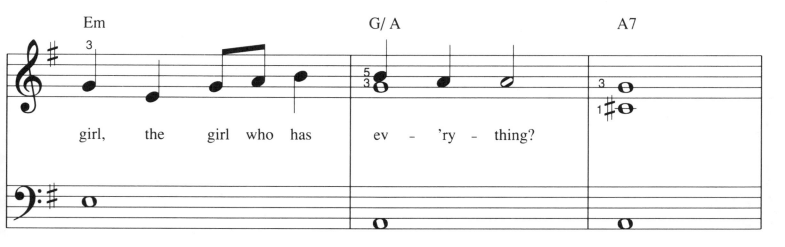

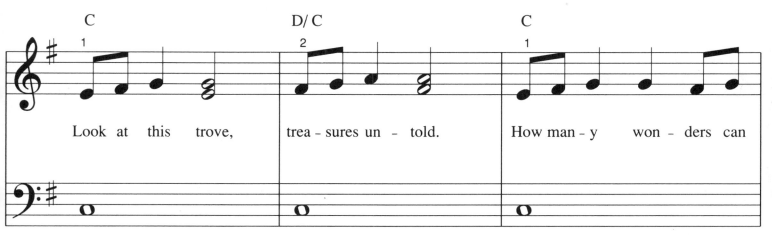

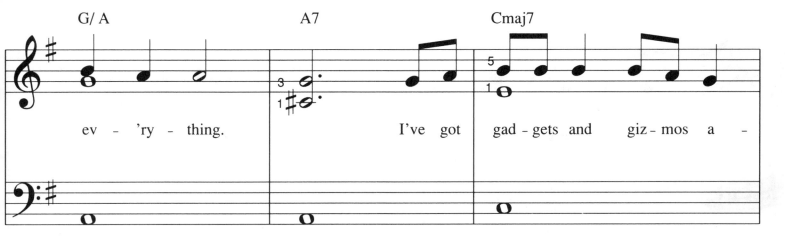

124

bove,

out of the sea.

slower

Wish I could be _____ part of that world.

L.H.

a tempo

SOMEDAY
from Walt Disney's THE HUNCHBACK OF NOTRE DAME

Music by ALAN MENKEN
Lyrics by STEPHEN SCHWARTZ

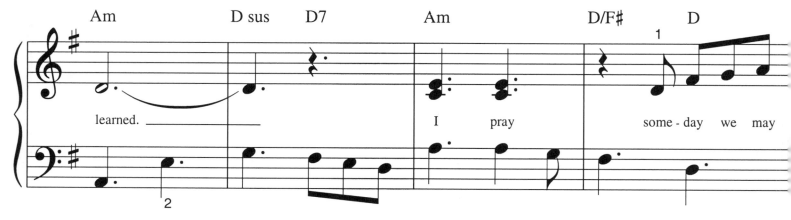

A SPOONFUL OF SUGAR
from Walt Disney's MARY POPPINS

Words and Music by RICHARD M. SHERMAN
and ROBERT B. SHERMAN

134

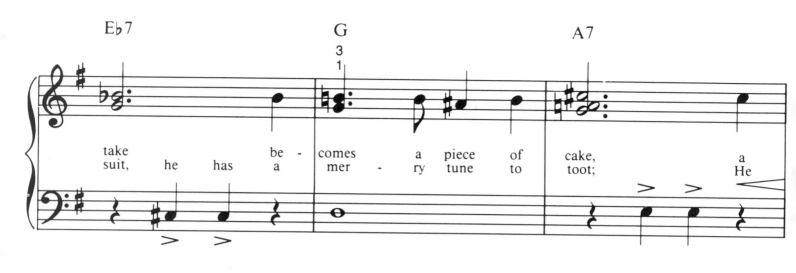

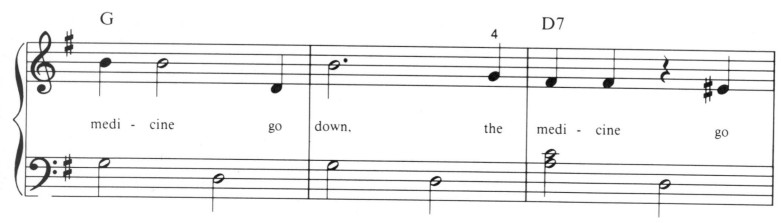

8va lower ⌐

SUPERCALIFRAGILISTIC-EXPIALIDOCIOUS

from Walt Disney's MARY POPPINS

Words and Music by RICHARD M. SHERMAN
and ROBERT B. SHERMAN

Brightly

139

TRUE TO YOUR HEART

from Walt Disney Pictures' MULAN

Music by MATTHEW WILDER
Lyrics by DAVID ZIPPEL

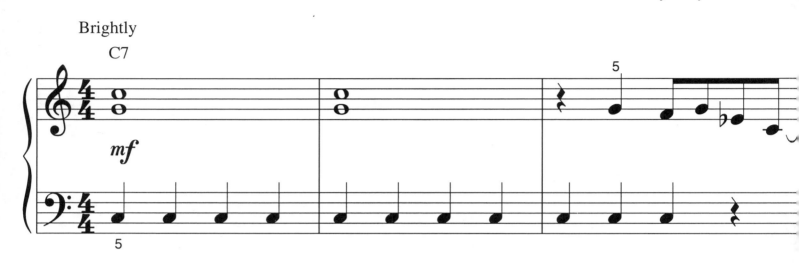

Ba - by, I knew at once that you were meant for me.

Deep in my soul, I know that I'm your des - ti - ny. Though

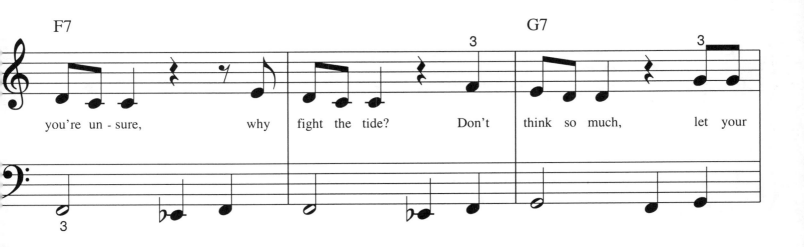

F7

you're un - sure, why fight the tide? Don't think so much, let your

G7

heart de - cide. _____

C7

Ba - by, I see your fu - ture, and it's
Some-one you know is on your side can

tied to mine. I
set you free. I can do that for you if you be-

look in your eyes and see you search - ing

F7

for a sign. But you'll
lieve in me. Why ____

nev - er fall 'til
sec - ond guess what

G7

you let go. ____ Don't
feels so right? ____ Just

be so scared of what
trust your heart and you'll

C

you don't ____ know.
see the ____ light.

True to your heart, you must be

Am

true to your heart. That's when the

F

heav-ens will part, and ba - by,

G7

show - er you with my love.

C

O - pen your eyes, your heart can

Am

tell you no lies. And when you're

F

true to your heart, I know it's

1.

G7

gon - na lead you straight to me. ____

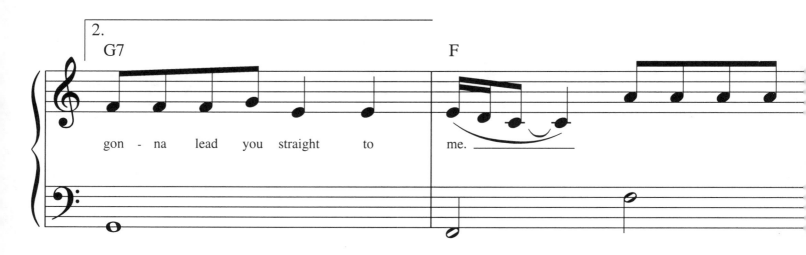

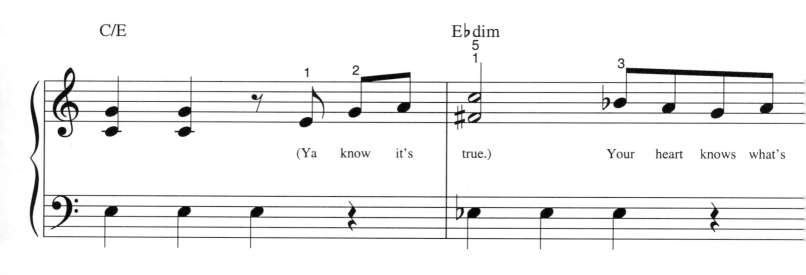

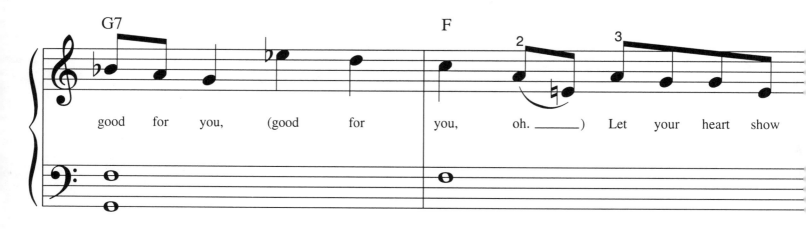

145

146

me. _____

When things are get-tin' cra-zy   and you don't know where to start, ___
When all the world a-round you,   it ___ seems to fall a-part, ___

keep on be - liev-ing, ba - by;   just be true to your heart.
keep on be - liev-ing, ba - by;   just be true to your heart.

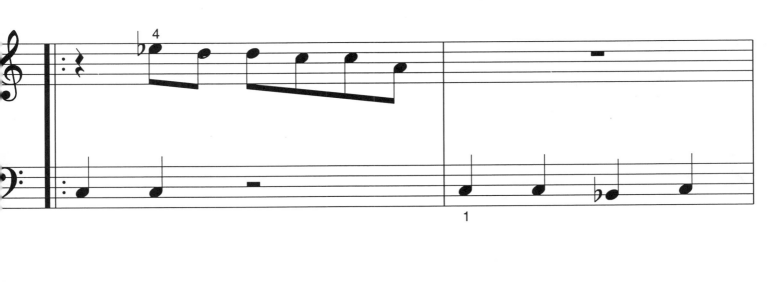

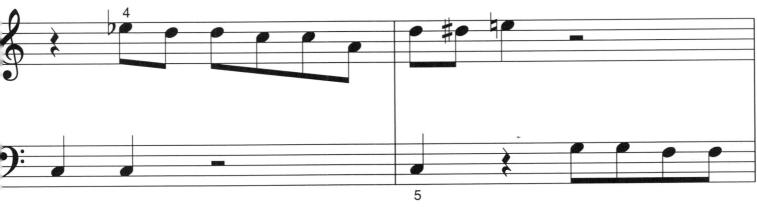

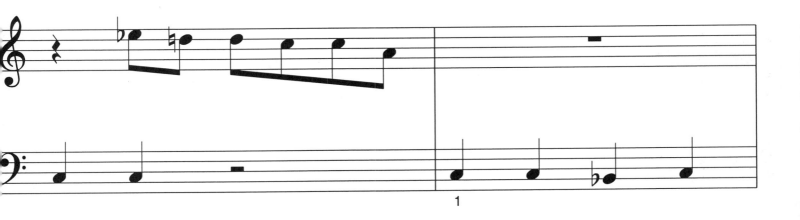

Repeat and Fade

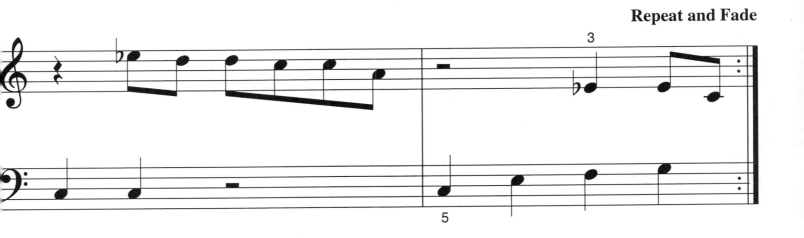

THE UNBIRTHDAY SONG
from Walt Disney's ALICE IN WONDERLAND

Words and Music by MACK DAVID
AL HOFFMAN and JERRY LIVINGSTON

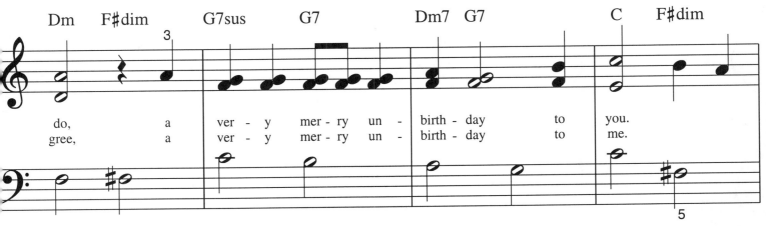

UNDER THE SEA
from Walt Disney's THE LITTLE MERMAID

Lyrics by HOWARD ASHMAN
Music by ALAN MENKEN

Brightly

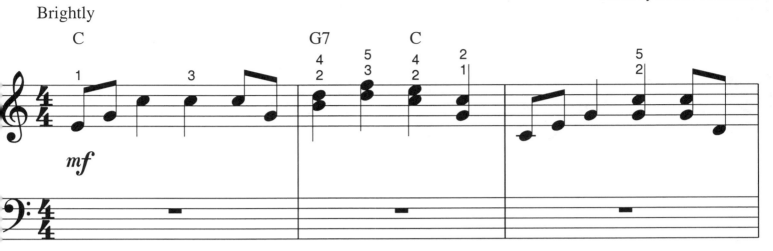

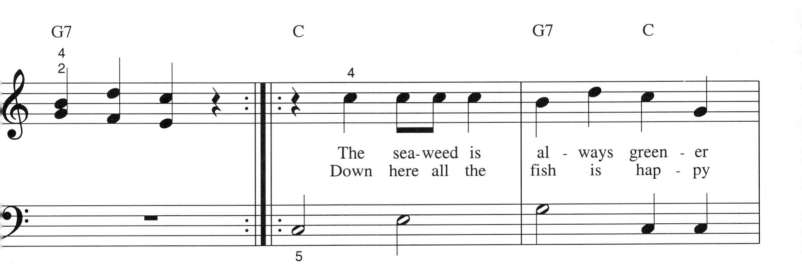

The sea-weed is al - ways green - er
Down here all the fish is hap - py

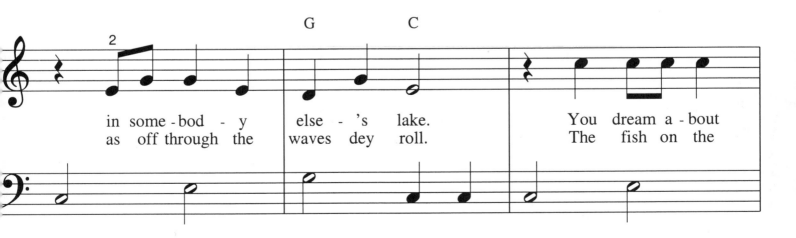

in some-bod - y else - 's lake.
as off through the waves dey roll.

You dream a - bout
The fish on the

G C   G C

go - ing   up   there.   But   that   is   a   big   mis - take.
land   ain't   hap - py.   They   sad   'cause they   in   the   bowl.

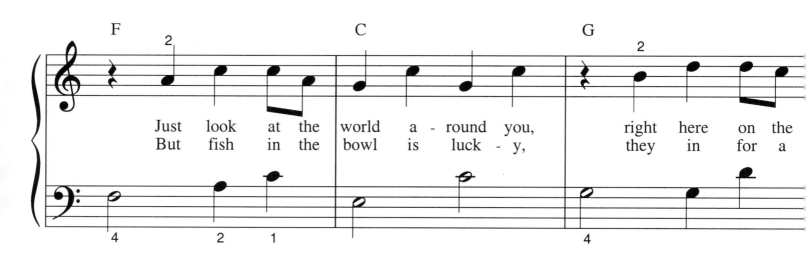

F   C   G

Just   look   at   the   world   a - round   you,   right   here   on   the
But   fish   in   the   bowl   is   luck - y,   they   in   for   a

o - cean   floor.

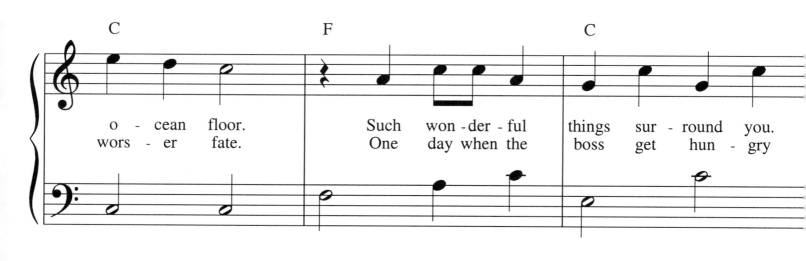

C   F   C

o - cean   floor.   Such   won - der - ful   things   sur - round   you.
wors - er   fate.   One   day   when   the   boss   get   hun - gry

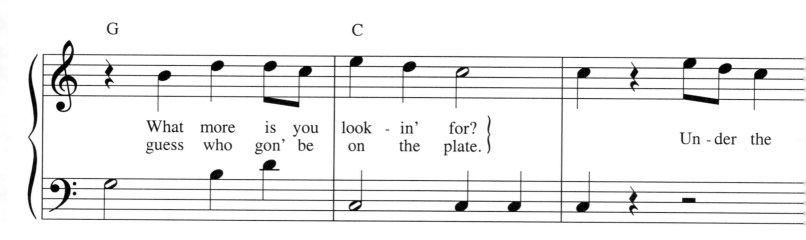

G   C

What   more   is   you   look - in'   for?   Un - der   the
guess   who   gon'   be   on   the   plate.

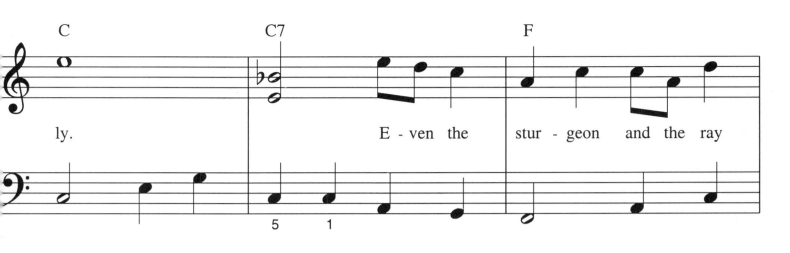

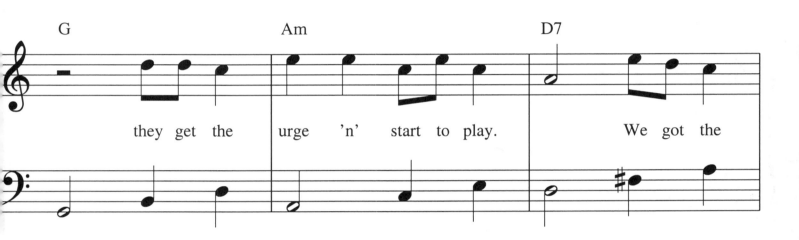

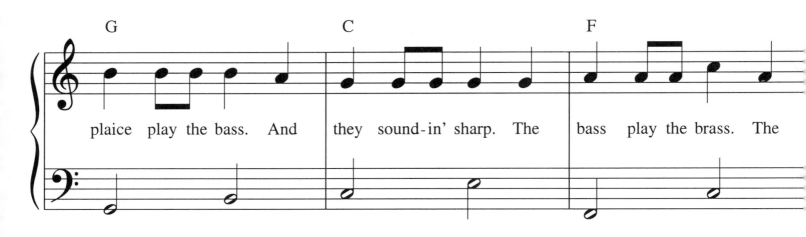

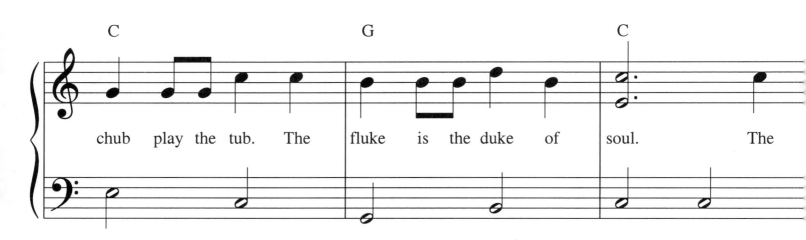

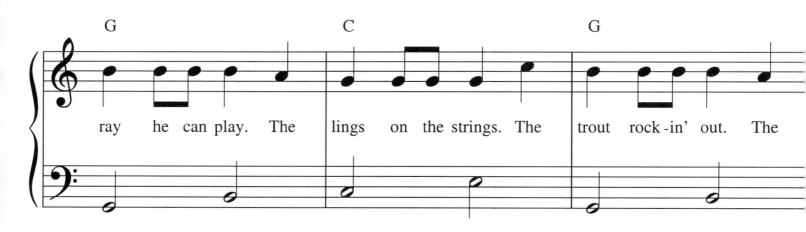

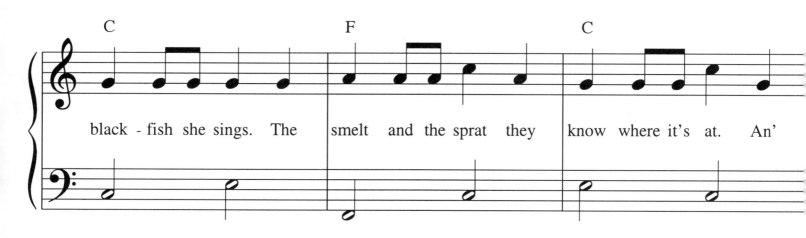

Oh,   that   blow - fish   blow.

Un - der the

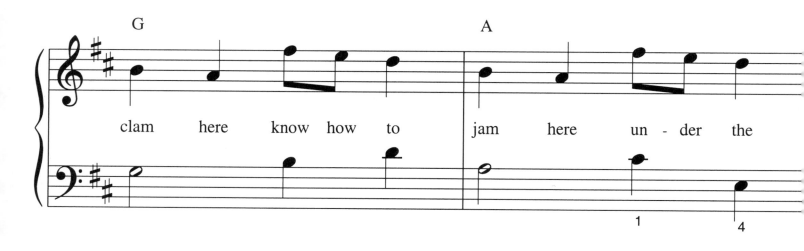

clam here know how to jam here un - der the

sea. Each lit - tle

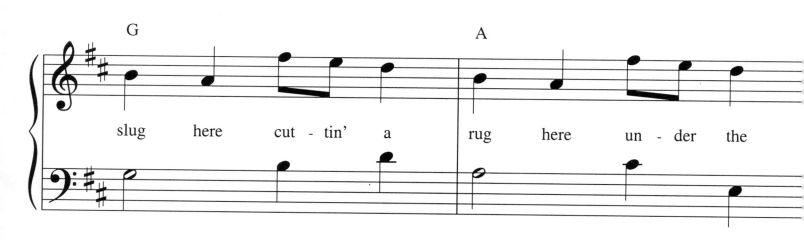

slug here cut - tin' a rug here un - der the

sea. Each lit - tle

A WHOLE NEW WORLD

from Walt Disney's ALADDIN

Music by ALAN MENKE

Lyrics by TIM RIC

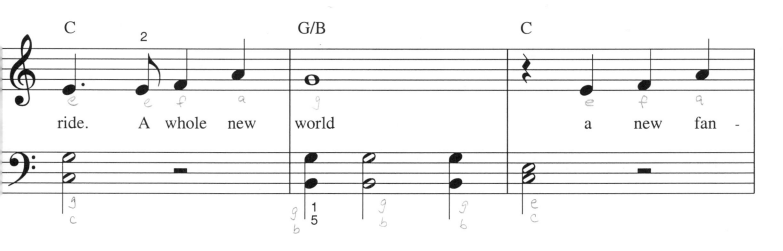

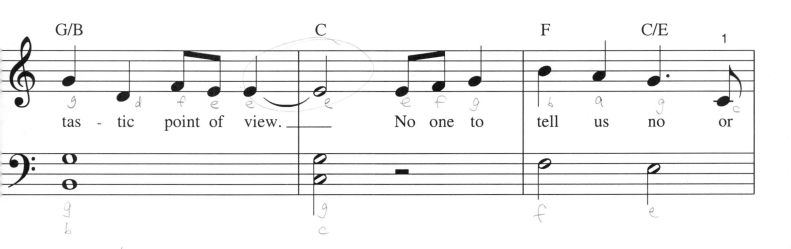

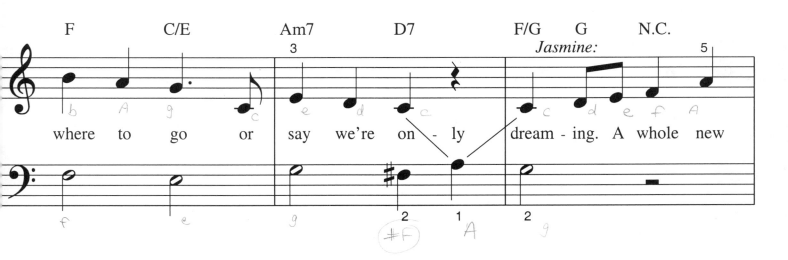

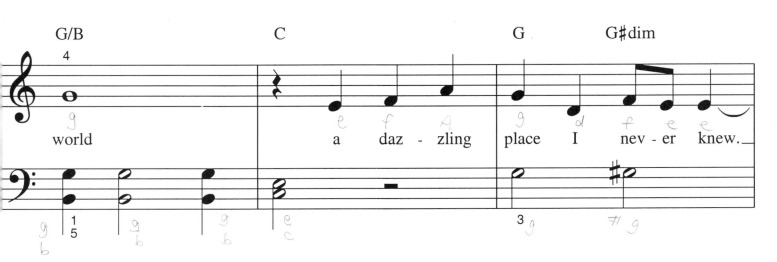

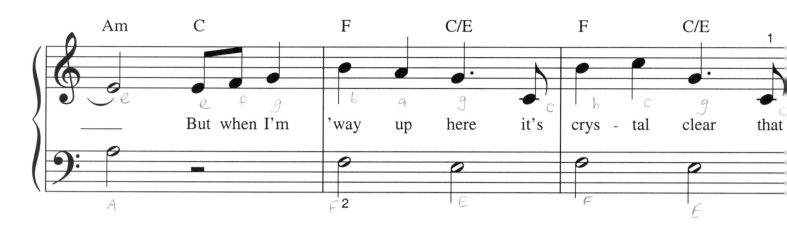

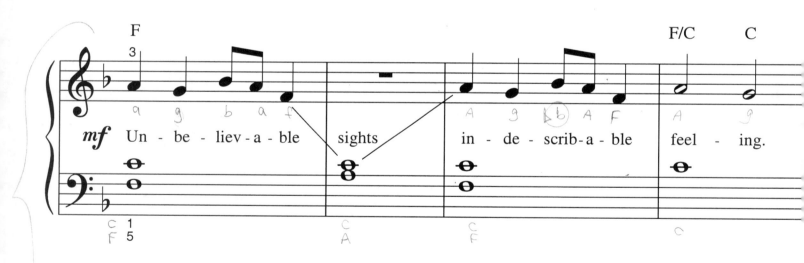

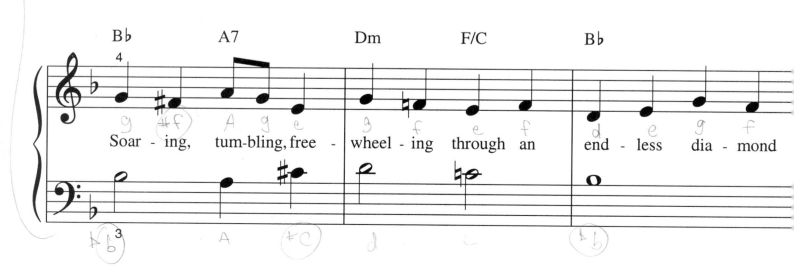

168

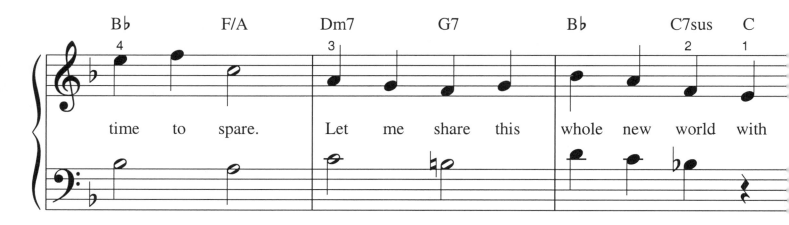

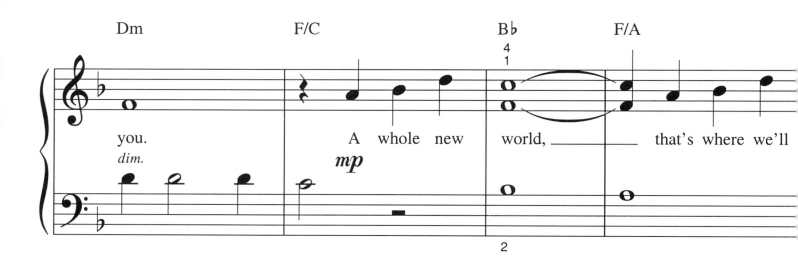

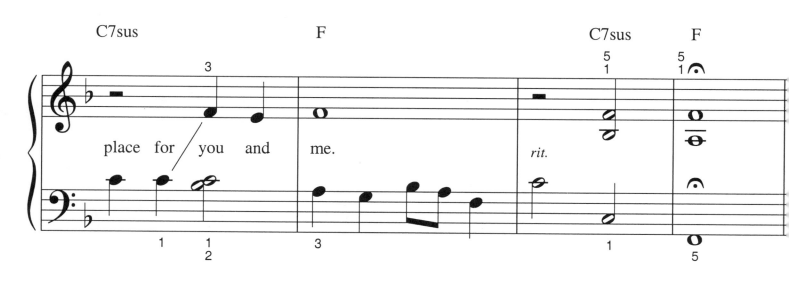

WINNIE THE POOH

from Walt Disney's THE MANY ADVENTURES OF WINNIE THE POOH

Words and Music by RICHARD M. SHERMAN
and ROBERT B. SHERMAN

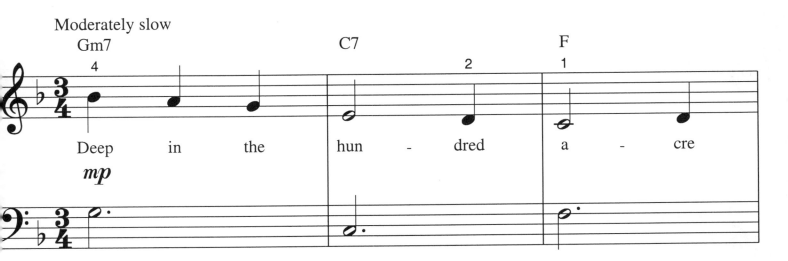

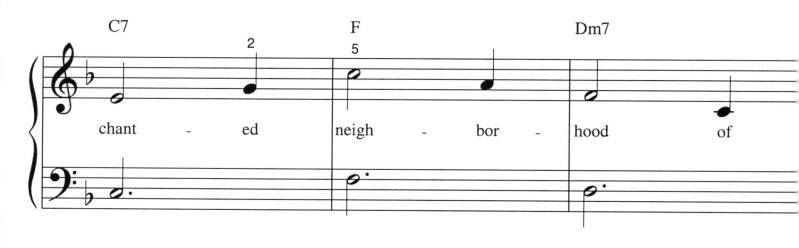

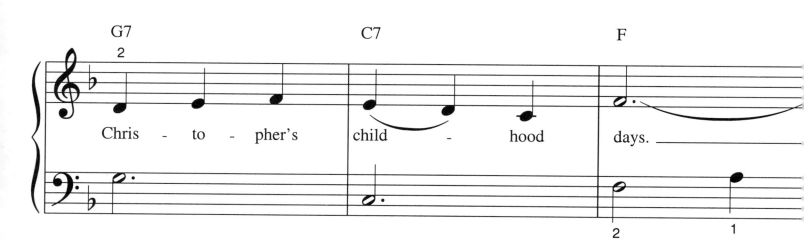

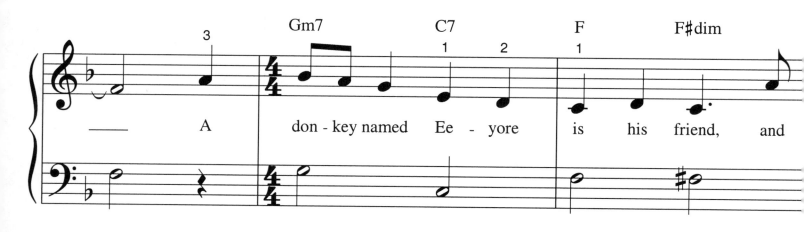

THE WONDERFUL THING
ABOUT TIGGERS

from Walt Disney's THE MANY ADVENTURES OF WINNIE THE POOH

Words and Music by RICHARD M. SHERMAN
and ROBERT B. SHERMAN

With a bounce (♩. = 1 beat)

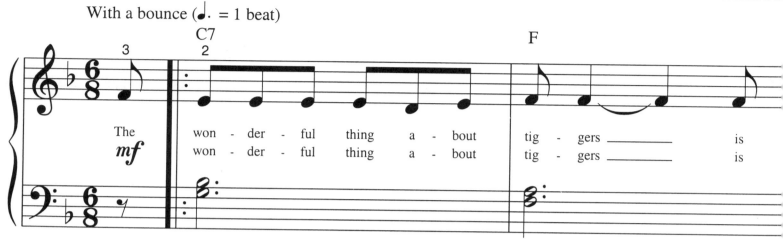

The / won - der - ful thing a - bout tig - gers _____ is
won - der - ful thing a - bout tig - gers _____ is

tig - gers are won - der - ful things! Their tops are made out of
tig - gers are won - der - ful chaps! They're loaded with vim and with

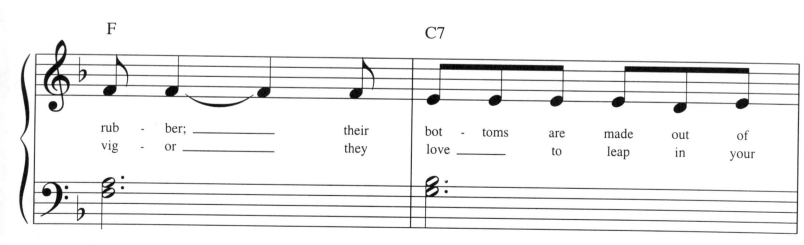

rub - ber; _____ their bot - toms are made out of
vig - or _____ they love ___ to leap in your

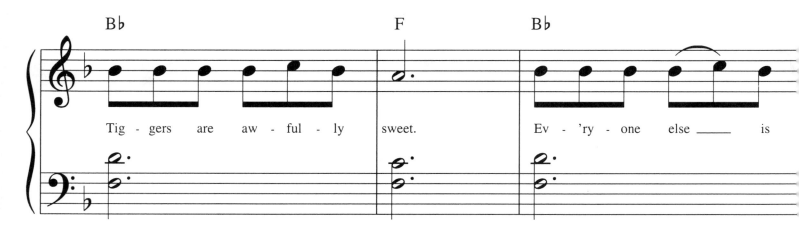

Tig - gers are aw - ful - ly sweet. Ev - 'ry - one else _____ is

jea - lous. _____ That's why I re - peat and re - peat: The

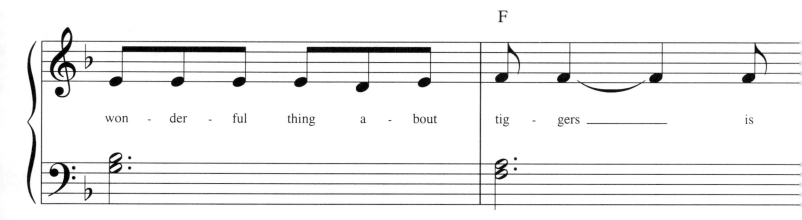

won - der - ful thing a - bout tig - gers _____ is

tig - gers are won - der - ful things! Their tops are made out of

YOU'LL BE IN MY HEART

(Pop Version)
from Walt Disney Pictures' TARZAN™

Words and Music
PHIL COLLIN

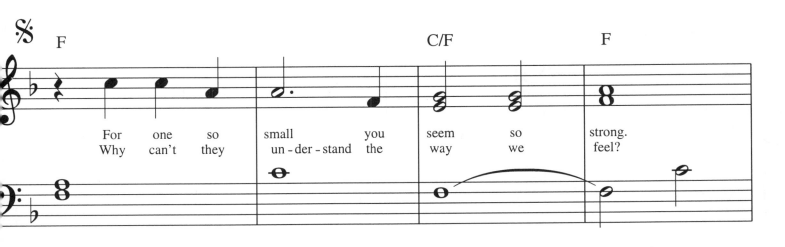

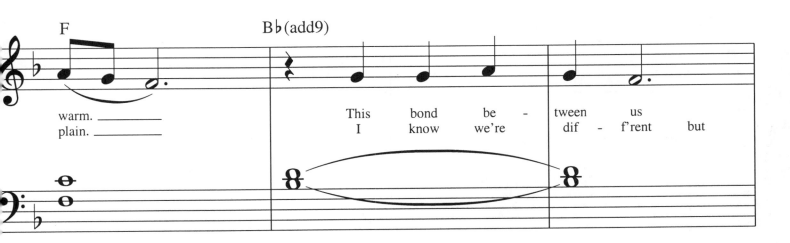

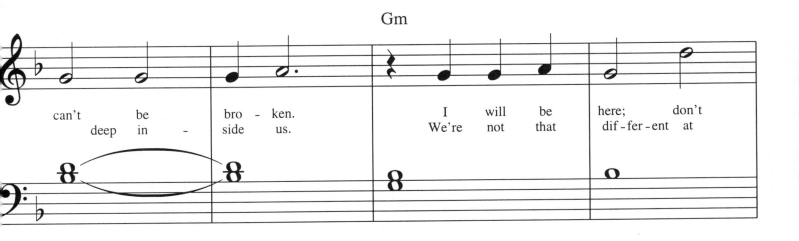

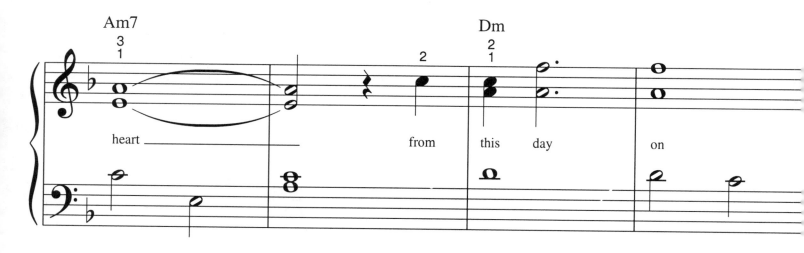

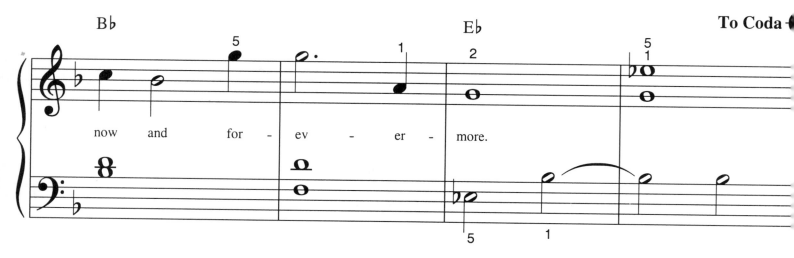

To Coda

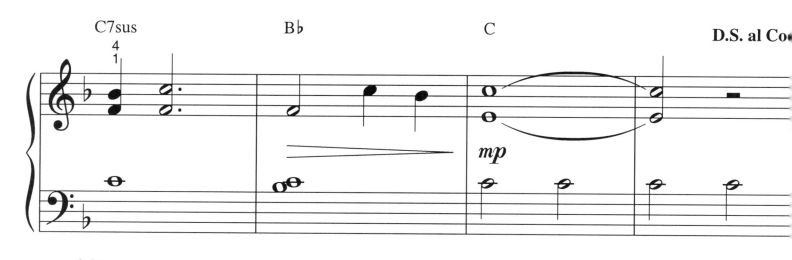

CODA

Don't lis - ten to them, ___
des - ti - ny calls ___

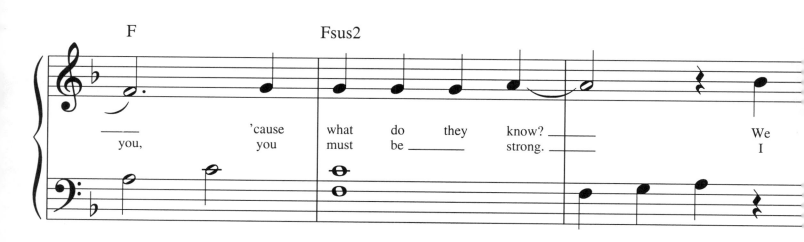

___ you, 'cause you what do they know? ___ We
you must be ___ strong. ___ I

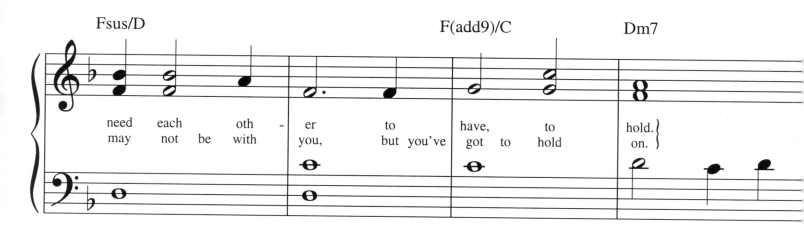

need each oth - er to have, to hold.
may not be with you, but you've got to hold on.

Am7

They'll   see   in   time,   I ___

1.
B♭

___   know. ___   When

2.
B♭   C

___   know. ___   We'll   show   them   to -

G   F

geth - er,   'cause   you'll   be   in ___   my ___

mf

184

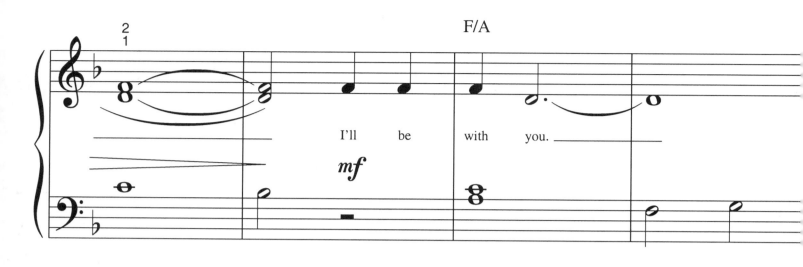

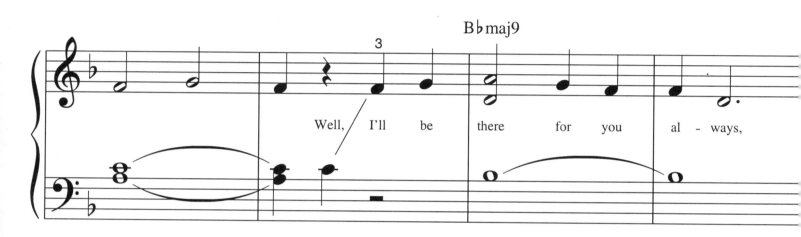

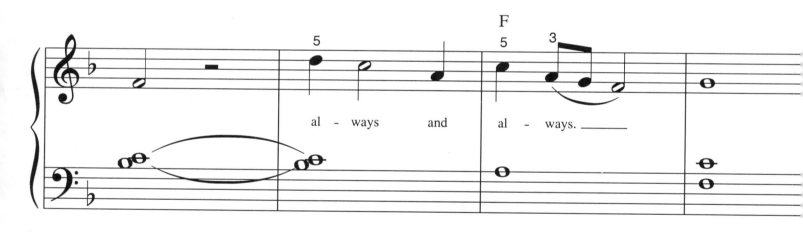

185

YOU'VE GOT A FRIEND IN ME

from Walt Disney's TOY STORY

Music and Lyrics by
RANDY NEWMAN

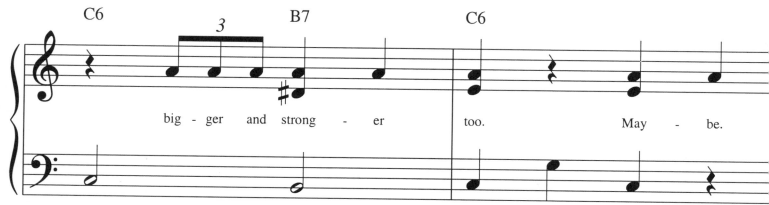

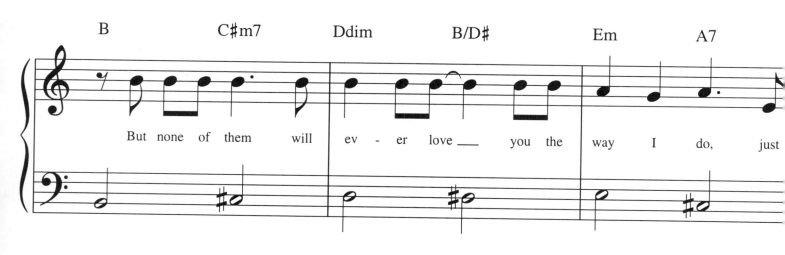

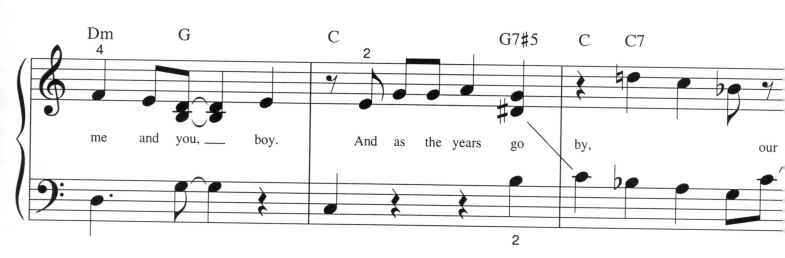

189

ZIP-A-DEE-DOO-DAH

from Walt Disney's SONG OF THE SOUTH

Words by RAY GILBER
Music by ALLIE WRUBE